HUGH REDWOOD

Hugh Redwood: With God in Fleet Street

by

WILLIAM CLARK

HODDER AND STOUGHTON
LONDON SYDNEY AUCKLAND TORONTO

To Jean

Author's Note

In the preparation of this biography I have been grateful for the information and inspiration provided by Hugh Redwood's own books. I am also deeply appreciative of the co-operation of Mrs. Elsie Redwood and Miss Gwen Redwood. The latter read the passages dealing with family relationships and happenings in the home, and I record my thanks herewith.

Salvation Army officers who worked alongside Hugh in the slums gave valuable information; their names appear in the text. Other people wrote me and shared memories; some sent letters. While all this material was not used it was all useful in contributing to the picture of Hugh Redwood's work and character I was forming in my mind. I am grateful to everyone.

Special thanks must go to Colonel John Hunt who not only coped magnificently with the burden of the typing, but who also assisted with some of the research.

Wm. C.

Contents

Turning Point

THERE WERE SOME unusually heavy falls of snow in the south of England during December 1927, and a number of people died from extreme cold, although Mr. Ingleby Oddie, the Westminster coroner, conducting the inquest of one unfortunate victim, said that 'in this country no man need die of cold, exposure or want of food. He need only apply to the nearest constable who will tell him where to obtain board and lodging free.'

The newspapers had pictures of cars buried deep in the snow, and there was one of a railway engine almost covered over. The River Stour was one mass of ice from Sandwich Toll Bridge to the Thames. One newspaper commented — and the words have a curiously modern ring! — 'There is little doubt now that the unusually severe and prolonged spell of wintry weather . . . caught the greater part of the country unawares.'

The forecasters announced that the extreme cold would persist and that 1927 would 'slide out'. In the event the New Year 'dripped in' as temperatures unexpectedly rose, and, with the ensuing thaw, the height of the country's rivers also. Severe flooding was reported in many places.

In London the Thames was badly affected and during the early morning of Saturday, January 7, an unusually high spring tide combined with strong winds and the flooded state of the river to produce a disaster of major proportions. In a number of areas from Hammersmith — where two women were drowned — to Dartford, the Thames overflowed and, in some places, broke its banks. The most serious breaches occurred in the Grosvenor Road district of Westminster where ten people lost their lives as the swirling black waters swept over the embankment and engulfed their little basement homes. Among the dead were four sisters ranging in age from eighteen to two and a half years. It was a heart-breaking sight for those who, at the call of duty or simply out of curiosity (and the disaster attracted many who just came to stare!), hurried to the spot. One eye-witness described what he saw:

Grosvenor Road reminded me of a thoroughfare in a French town which had been heavily bombarded by artillery and aeroplanes. (The First World War had ended less than ten years before.) The devastation was unbelievable. Hundreds of tons of masonry, part of a strong containing wall of the Thames, were scattered in all directions, the surface of the road was completely wrecked and thousands of paving stones were lying about as though they had been blown up by a terrific explosion. I picked up a child's exercise book containing an essay on the Thames. In it the following occurred: *'The river was used by the Romans and is still used by English people and is known as Father Thames because he is so kind to us and has made the city of London possible.'* It was heart-breaking to go along North Street, Causton Street, Hinchcliffe Street, Ponsonby Place, Ponsonby Road and Vincent Street. Everywhere I felt the presence of death. At all houses the blinds were drawn, either because tragedy had overtaken occupants or as a token of sorrow for the bereaved. The furniture was either totally destroyed or badly damaged and one saw scores of families reduced to a pitiable sight. I saw cart after cart calling at these basement dwellings, taking what was worth being removed to a place of safety. The carts were followed by weeping women, some with children in their arms, while men had bundles slung over their shoulders. The procession was like a line of refugees escaping from a city threatened by a foreign foe. (*Daily News*)

This was an important story, chock full of drama, of human interest, and it was scooped by the now defunct London newspaper, the *Daily News*, when three of its editorial workers, travelling home in the early hours of the morning, their spell of night duty completed, found that their usual tramway service, which ran by the way of the Thames embankment, was disrupted. They soon discovered the reason: the tracks were awash with muddy water. What did this mean? Was there a story here? They could not possibly have dreamed how big a story they had in fact chanced upon. Urgent enquiries revealed something of the truth and, in the best traditions of a profession which calls for initiative and prompt action, the newspaper men, forgetting about home and bed, set about organising the news for immediate publication, though they very well knew that the final edition of their paper had already gone to press. They hurried back to their offices, despatched one of their number by taxi to the Grosvenor Road district where, it was said, the disaster was most serious, and began to set up a special late London edition to carry the news. It was printed at four-thirty. As the night editor remarked, in recounting the occasion years later, it was 'an outstandingly smart piece of work'.

* * *

This man, Hugh Redwood — and it is his story which is being told in this book — had every reason to be pleased with those who had pulled off so remarkable a scoop, and pleased with himself also. Though he personally had had little to do with it, having left his office around midnight for his home in the suburbs after the manner of night editors when it seemed that little of importance was brewing, he was nevertheless technically responsible, and could legitimately take credit for what had been achieved by his men. So the taste of success — his paper's success — was sweet when, over his toast and marmalade, he opened his copy early next morning. The main news page lay-out which he himself had prepared was not there. It had been scrapped, and only one thing could justify a procedure of that kind — a big news story. And there it was in black and white. It was indeed a scoop.

Recalling his deep sense of satisfaction, he said that whereas the other night editors overturned their breakfast trays that morning as they leapt out of bed to the telephone with their eyes a-goggle over what they had just glimpsed in a rival sheet, his own thrill was of an order more pleasant and his own conversation over the telephone sweetened by the knowledge that the glory of the scoop was his vicariously because his own 'boys' had put it over. (*God in the Slums*)

That day, Saturday, was the one free day of his working week. His plans were made. He would visit his daughter,

Gwen, who was a patient in a London hospital, then travel home to spend the day in blissful relaxation. But while he was seated in his home-bound train discovering in the evening edition of his paper (printed around noon!) how the big story was developing, the sense of satisfaction which had come to him with the scoop that was theirs, and which had been with him all morning, gave way to feelings of sympathy for the victims of the disaster. Up till now he had given them little thought as people. He was a journalist and to him it was the story that mattered. But he well knew that while the ability to see life as news is the first of good qualities in a journalist, in the absence of a powerful corrective it may, and quite frequently does become a curse, a constant menace to sincerity.

So now the magnitude of the human tragedy of the Westminster floods hit him like a sledge-hammer — ten people drowned, all loved by someone, each leaving a gap, and many more rendered homeless, having lost all the worldly goods they possessed. And though in some cases those worldly goods were pitifully few, they were treasured nevertheless. Years later he recorded that he thought he could go to the very spot in Burnt Ash Hill, Lee, to the very paving stone, a few yards from the Crown Hotel and almost within the sight of his own front door, where he had stopped and decided to return to London, to Westminster, and involve himself somehow in the need the disaster had brought.

He acted on an impulse, and the passing of time confirmed that he was right, so very right, to do so. That decision changed the whole of his life and opened up for him experiences which at that moment he could not possibly have imagined. It was a turning point.

*   *   *

When Hugh arrived at Westminster he kept a look out for the uniform of The Salvation Army, for that Movement's work in the disaster had been reported, and quickly located Major Mary Patch and two of her helpers, Captain Lucy Warren and Lieutenant May Collingbourne, the latter having just recently graduated from the Army's training college for officers. He noticed one striking difference in the uniforms they were wearing from those he had seen before when he had encountered Salvation Army women. Whereas he had been accustomed to the bonnet with the red ribbon, the women working at Westminster wore mushroom-shaped hats which in the 1970s would almost certainly have made their wearers objects of fun, but which even in 1928 were hardly the height of fashion. He later learned that this distinctive headgear identified the wearers as members of the Slum Department (as it was then called) of the Army's operations. This meant not only that they worked in the slum areas but lived there also, two or three to a post, right in among the poverty-stricken people they were pledged to help; help, that is, towards Christ, the motive and aim of all their activities, and also with every conceivable problem that could arise. In the slums these were many and varied.

As he got to know the 'Slums' (for that appellation, he was told by a girl-Lieutenant, described not only *where* they worked but *the workers themselves*), his admiration for them and their self-sacrificing work amid indescribable conditions and in all manner of circumstances, was to increase, so much so that he was to count it a privilege over many years to have some share in their endeavours. But at this point of meeting it was their businesslike appearance and deportment, their devotion and sincerity, the calmly confident way in which they were coming to grips with the tragic situation, that impressed him.

He begged Major Patch to allow him to help. Almost as soon as he had arrived at the spot he had been glad to hand her his own new note-book when he saw that all she had was a stub of pencil and a piece of brown paper. He wanted to do more. He asked for a job. Just then a horse and van appeared bearing a sack of unmistakably second-hand clothing for distribution to the flood victims. A girl-Lieutenant dragged the heavy bundle out and it was then the Major said to the waiting man: 'I wonder if you would help the Lieutenant to carry the sack into the next street?' He was 'in' with the Slums!

A relationship began there and then in that London street that was to develop through the years, and lead the night editor into such God-honouring adventures in service to the needy, that many would rise up and call him blessed. It was to all this as yet hidden activity that Hugh Redwood turned when, almost within sight of his own front door, he set his face towards Westminster and the floods.

CHAPTER I

Beginnings

THE ONLY CHILD of 'good, average, middle-class, churchgoing parents' — his own description — Hugh Redwood (christened William Arthur Hugh) was born on February 15, 1883. His grandfather was the smithy in the village of Uplowman, five miles from Tiverton in Devon, but early on his son William, Hugh's father, decided that the life of a village blacksmith was not for him, and he betook himself to the city of Exeter and secured a post as compositor with the *Exeter Gazette*. That was how he came to meet the girl who became his wife.

Though barely eighteen herself she appears to have possessed more culture, more worldly wisdom than the lad from the country, and she took it upon herself to lead him into the ways of self-improvement. He began to learn shorthand and became so proficient that he was eventually known as one of the best exponents of the art in the whole of the West Country. In time he graduated from the compositors' to the reporters' room and was chief reporter on the *Western Daily Press*, of Bristol, when he died in 1918, after having held the position for forty-two years. That length of time in one post is probably an indication of the truth of the observation that Hugh made later that his father was not a greatly ambitious man. Some of the young journalists who passed through his hands did brilliantly in London and elsewhere, but the big city held no attraction for him. When Hugh opened his father's weekly pay packet after his death it contained only five gold sovereigns.

* * *

Hugh left on record thoughts regarding his relationship with his parents and it is plain that his father made the greater impression upon him. When he started out to work it was as a cub reporter on the newspaper with which his father was, and had been for some years, associated. This, as Hugh confessed, had quite serious drawbacks. If, in the course of his duties, the father had reserved for his son too many of the more enviable reporting assignments — those out-of-town jobs with which there went larger than usual expense accounts — some of Hugh's colleagues would have been quick to accuse him of receiving too many favours. The outcome was that few of the better jobs ever came to him.

In other ways Hugh thought that his father was *too* considerate, when he should have exercised firmer discipline. But he also felt he watched over his progress in journalism as though he were living his own life over again, glad to see his son having chances he himself never had.

The father taught the son many things, the greatest of which was the fact that the newspaper man must learn that it is the news that matters, first, last and always. Hugh commented that as a journalist he felt he owned more than he could explain to a mentor who had impressed him with this great truth.

Hugh achieved a great deal in his profession. He may not

have been willing to include himself among the brilliant men his father had launched on their careers — Hugh Redwood was too modest for that — but his achievements were not small. Perhaps, if he had not become so involved in the work of The Salvation Army, and in other religious endeavours, they might have been greater. As it was he became successively foreign editor and night editor of the *Daily News*, and later the night editor of the *News Chronicle* — when that paper came into being with the amalgamation of the *Daily News* and the *Daily Chronicle*. Later still he became deputy editor and then religious editor. The latter post was created for him and was the one he held when he retired in 1953 after fifty-five years in journalism.

There was another reason why his father made a greater impression upon him than did his mother. His father lived longer. Whereas Hugh was not quite twenty-one when his mother died, he was a married man with his own family when his father fell victim to the influenza epidemic which in 1918 was sweeping around the world. He weakened himself by overstrain, turning out night after night to do the work of younger men who had been taken ill. Eventually, after returning home from another's reporting engagement in the cold and rain on top of an open tram car, he caught the disease himself. Hugh watched over him for two nights before the end came. He later described his father's death as 'the one dark shadow' to fall upon him in a particularly happy period in both his professional and family life.

Hugh had many pleasant memories of the years when his father was still with him, following his mother's death. Even after the younger man moved to London he saw a great deal of his father, for Bristol was not far away by train. Later still, during a period in the early days of the First World War when Hugh, with his wife and daughter, lived in Herne Bay, Redwood Senior often spent a weekend with them and occasionally joined them for a holiday. The young married man was often glad of his father's advice in many matters, including the managing of the household budget. Hugh considered that it was during those years that they got to know each other best. 'His was a strong arm on which to lean,' he wrote later, recalling an uncertain period in his own life, 'and I was grateful for his silences.'

Hugh's relationship with his mother does not ever seem to have been close, despite the fact that in his early years he was with her frequently. Indeed, during his teenage years, owing to his father's preoccupation with work, he was often his mother's escort, accompanying her to concerts, the theatre and the like, for which she had a marked predilection. They were more like brother and sister than mother and son. Yet there was no real *rapport* between them, though he desperately wanted to know her more deeply. Often a great longing would come over him, a passionate desire, to throw his arms around her, bury his face in her dress, and give her kiss for kiss. But there was nothing there for him, only the breath of violets, her favourite flower, a bunch of which she often had at her waist. There was nothing there for him to love. A few years before she died, at the early age of forty-six, they began, as Hugh put it, to 'drift out of sympathy' and 'into conflict'. He stood dry-eyed before her open grave, he wrote, saddened and softened by the knowledge that they had finally eluded one another. Wishing he had known her better, he gently tossed a little bunch of violets on to her coffin. 'Violets', he said, 'for loneliness.'

* * *

Hugh's parents were sincerely religious people, though that appeared to mean only that they were regular attenders at church, that they had their son baptised, that his mother taught him to say simple prayers and his grace before meals, and that she herself told him such Bible stories as she considered suitable. No doubt in these days, when the majority do not attend church, so much would mark out a family in the community as most definitely — and perhaps even oddly — religious. But Hugh, who was later to undergo that life-changing experience we call conversion, did not consider that his parents' endeavours secured him a *spiritual* education. They practised *religion*, sincerely no doubt, but only as part of that middle-class respectability they seemed so anxious to preserve.

When he was old enough Hugh became a member of the choir of the Anglican Church of St. Andrew, in Bristol. But, he confessed, 'if there is any one tribe of boys more peculiarly devilish than any other it is the tribe that veils its iniquities beneath the choir-boys' robes of innocence'. If we might hesitate to apply that to church choirs everywhere, Hugh had no doubt regarding the group of which he was a member. Most of the boys, he said frankly, were young heathens, their morals low, and their language at times appalling, and his joining them worked only to the serious detriment of his soul.

But he did see real religion in Annie Tye. Annie was a maid in the Redwood household and she had a great deal to do with Hugh's early upbringing. She was chapel, whereas the Redwoods were church. She sang Moody and Sankey; her employers sang Hymns Ancient and Modern. This was in the days of Victoria when people gathered around the organ or piano in their homes, especially on Sundays; radio and television were yet far in the future.

Hugh learned about Annie's choice of hymns, not because she sang them during the course of her duties — she would never have been allowed to practise such an extravagance — but because sometimes, on her days off, she would take Hugh to her parents' home, and it was there, to the accompaniment of an American organ, that they would all sing. Annie's father's favourites were hymns with a nautical flavour: 'Let the lower lights be burning' and, 'Pull for the shore, sailor', which the Bristol boy, with the love of the sea in his blood, could very properly appreciate.

Annie also told Hugh Bible stories and, unlike his mother, she told them in vivid colours so that they came alive for him. He remembered them, while he forgot his mother's. Annie's religion was simple — and real. She believed in the Bible and practised its teachings. Hugh said he was indebted to her for much, and not least for showing him how religion ought to be related to all of life.

But, alas, even Annie's wholesome influence did not ensure any steady progress of the boy towards the good. Maybe the girl left the household early, for there are no references to her when Hugh writes of his later boyhood years, and by the time he reached his teens it would appear that her good influence was no longer having any effect.

* * *

Hugh left school with no real religion, though it was a cathedral school and though he had been confirmed at the age of thirteen. He did leave, however, with a love for music; that much did his cathedral-school education impart to him. He revelled in Stainer and Barnaby. But when he joined the paper of which his father was the chief reporter, at a salary of ten shillings

(50p) a week, he joined as he put it, 'an educational establishment of a very different order'.

One of the duties that fell to Hugh's lot during the first two years of his employment was the reporting of inquests. The days were rare, he recalled, which did not bring at least one such assignment his way, and on one 'depressing' Friday, he had to attend no fewer than thirteen. Those two years left an impression on his character which he did not lose in twenty years.

Brought face to face with death, often in mysterious and tragic circumstances (though, it ought to be said, the reporter did not, as a rule, actually see the body) — Hugh found it became commonplace; sympathies, conscience and sensitivity were dulled. Death seemed to him a 'random, wanton thing' and difficult to reconcile with theories of a loving God.

Long before he left school, it had been his practice to recite the Apostles' Creed regularly. He had to; his duties as a choir boy demanded it. But it meant little to him; he hardly gave any thought to it. There was no denial of God, no stated unbelief, but there was no real faith either. He still said his prayers, because he always had and he remained in the choir; but there was nothing resembling an authentic personal experience of Christ.

Concurrent with this vague belief went the developing of habits which, at the time, were to him signs of his maturing manhood, but which in reality were evidences of the rapidity with which he was going the wrong way.

At eighteen, he later frankly confessed, he could smoke stronger cigars and use stronger language than his father, keep worse hours than his mother, and make more profit out of his reporter's expenses sheet than the most brazen of his seniors.

On one occasion, worse for drink, he had to be escorted home by a policeman and it was only because the law-man was a good sort and knew Hugh's father, that there was no prosecution. Hugh was very quickly acquiring a fund of knowledge about the seamier side of life. Long before he was twenty-one he reckoned he was a man, and by some standards he was. Where he might have landed had something quite remarkable not happened to him we shall never know. But he met and joined The Salvation Army.

* * *

We must see in a moment how this came to pass, but before we do we should go back a few years to meet his Great Aunt Elizabeth. This estimable, if (so far as the Redwoods were concerned) slightly eccentric lady was Hugh's father's aunt. She had fallen on somewhat difficult times, but she lived near her relatives in Bristol and they had taken it upon themselves to keep an eye on her. It was Hugh's duty every Sunday to take her her dinner and he was made well aware of what he considered her strangeness as he shared a cup of tea with her — which he was always constrained to do — and viewed with some amusement the navy-blue, red-ribboned bonnet which hung from a nail on the wall. Great Aunt Elizabeth was a Salvationist.

Hugh suffered these enforced visits on Sundays, but he was always glad to get away. He would have been more uncomfortable still had he known what his great aunt thought about him. Many years later he learned this from a retired Salvation Army officer who, as a girl, used to visit Elizabeth every week with a copy of The Salvation Army's newspaper, *The War Cry*. They used to talk together a good deal and it seems that the main topic of the old lady's conversation was her great nephew. She considered him a veritable sinner, bound for eternal damnation, and she prayed long and earnestly for him. When Hugh learned this in later life he knew what was one of the important factors in his conversion: his great aunt's prayers.

But, so far as he was then concerned, when his conversion took place the main cause, on the earthly level, was the heart-searching address of another woman-Salvationist.

In the days of Hugh Redwood's youth, sermons were still good copy for the local newspaper. More often than not the church services which were noticed in the advertisement columns on Saturday were reported in the new columns on Monday. Along with his colleagues Hugh was frequently assigned to such reporting engagements. They were not often warmly accepted, but had to be tolerated as part of the job. He would sit in the church and listen, because his job depended on it. But the listening and the writing were performed professionally; few of the preacher's words made an impression on his mind — except what was necessary to enable him to furnish an acceptable report — and certainly not on his heart.

But one Sunday morning in January 1901, a church reporting assignment came his way which turned out to be different, so different that for some time, as a result of it, the direction of his life was changed. He was sent by his father to report a service to be conducted in the Broadmead Baptist Church, Bristol, by Florence Booth, wife of Bramwell Booth, who later became the Army's second General. It was a salutary experience. He did not in after life remember what she said but there was at one and the same time a disturbing and, as with John Wesley, a heart-warming experience he could not explain. It made him abandon his note-taking and listen eagerly. When, at the conclusion of the service, he walked out into the raw, damp air the glow in his heart was undiminished. He went home in a state of rare excitement.

That evening he encountered a uniformed Salvationist in the street and ventured to speak to him about his experience, and was properly told, without any hint of embarrassment, and with a marked absence of cant that impressed him, that the Spirit of God was obviously dealing with him. He was given an invitation to attend the meeting that was to be held in the Salvation Army hall the next evening. He went, and though so much seemed strange to him, even ridiculous, it was there and then, in that meeting, that he went forward to kneel at the Penitent-form. The 'Hallelujahs' of the Salvationists were loud and sincere. Writing later of the experience Hugh said that for the first time, in spite of all his previous religious activity, he felt that Christ was a present reality; he felt that he was there and then offered a completely new way of life, and he accepted it gratefully.

His decision was not well received at home. His mother's distress, especially when later he bought and wore Salvation Army uniform, was most marked. Indeed, for a short time he was compelled to leave home, but went back when his parents calmed down a little, though they never came to terms with their son's new way of life.

Had they known, of course, how short-lived the episode would be, they most likely would not have worried so much, but before he fell away he entered with such enthusiasm into all kinds of Salvationist activity that they must have felt he was in it for life.

*   *   *

Because he was a good 'catch', Hugh was much encouraged by the Ensign, the man-officer in charge of the Salvation Army corps. When he was put up to speak in indoor and outdoor meetings, as he often was, he was announced as 'the converted reporter'. He was in time invited to travel with more experienced Salvationists to other places to help with the leading of meetings, and he even considered seriously whether he ought to offer for Salvation Army officership. He might have done this had not the Ensign under whom he had been converted, and who had taken so great an interest in him, been given 'Farewell Orders', and moved to another corps. The man who followed him was of a different sort. He and Hugh did not see eye to eye and before long Hugh was out. Soon he was smoking and drinking again and trying to forget the experience of the previous twelve months.

Years later, reflecting on the real reasons for his relapse — for he knew it went deeper than a personality clash with the new officer — Hugh did not excuse himself from blame. Nothing, he wrote, could justify what he did. His defection was a deliberate act on his part. Nevertheless, he felt three other factors contributed to his downfall. In the first place he felt he was given too much publicity at the beginning; the Salvationists sought to exploit their unusual convert, though doubtless from the highest motives. And all that was not good for him.

The second and third reasons, he said, were more serious: a lack of teaching on prayer, and failure to relate holiness to daily life and work. What he needed and did not receive, was instruction in communion with God. Instead he was thrown into an endless round of evangelistic activity that did little for his own growth in grace.

His indictment should be a salutary warning to all who are charged with the responsibility of nurturing converts in the faith. Reflection should show that Hugh Redwood was indeed right in observing that failure to teach and develop the inner life of the soul is a serious matter.

So Hugh's early experience with The Salvation Army was really only a mild flirtation that lasted just over a year. But as the chapter closed he could not have imagined how dramatically it was to open again thirty years later, when he renewed his association with the Movement in which he had first felt the stirrings of real spiritual life. But this is part of his later story. In the meantime his mind turned towards London.

CHAPTER 2

To London

WHEN HUGH SECURED a job in Fleet Street in 1905, he fulfilled an ambition that had been his for some years; it was only because his parents had been against the idea that he had put it to the back of his mind. But now that his mother was dead, bringing, as he put it, a 'consequent change in the home', the old longing came upon him again. And having come of age he was in a position to please himself.

There was also something else. The previous summer, while on holiday in Ilfracombe, he had met and fallen in love with Edith, and Edith was from London. What further confirmation did he need that London was now the place for him?

Edith worked with a girl who had a link, through a cousin, with someone in Fleet Street, and word was passed to Hugh that there was a vacancy in the Central News Agency for a sub-editor. (A news agency is a wholesaler of news). He promptly made his application, was summoned from Bristol for an interview and was given the job on the spot at three pounds a week. That was considerably more than he was receiving as a reporter with the *Western Daily Press*, and as there was a promise of a rise to three guineas after a satisfactory trial period, and the possibility of a further rise to five pounds, future prospects were bright.

Hugh was to be with Central News for the next thirteen years. He called them his 'formative years', for during that time he greatly widened his experience of journalism, especially in the realm of foreign affairs. Encouraged by Edith, he worked hard to improve his facility with French and to acquire some knowledge of German and Spanish. These painstaking endeavours, plus his study of foreign news, were, he said, the makings of him. When, years later, the *Daily News* wanted a foreign editor and diplomatic correspondent, Hugh was ready and able.

* * *

For the first few years, until he married, he was engaged chiefly on night work, but that was no hardship. Often, he said, when the pressure of work had eased a little, he would leave the office for a few minutes and go out into the night air, savouring the silence, which was only occasionally broken by a late (or perhaps early!) hansom cab rattling by. He enjoyed having the place to himself much as, as he put it, one enjoys having one's home back again when the guests have gone away after a noisy house party.

His new work was varied and interesting. Because the agency worked with agents and correspondents in many lands, the translating of telegrams and cables from other parts of the world was an important part of the job and as Hugh was reputed to be good at French, the language the agency most frequently employed, he was kept busy.

His first translation assignment, given him by John

Gennings, one of the three Johns who ran Central News — the others were John Moore and John Lanyon — was an experience he did not soon forget. The truth of it was that he was not really up to it; his knowledge of French was not as great as he had supposed — as he saw immediately the sheets for translation were handed to him. There were ten pages, all printed in capitals, with most of the small words omitted and without a single stop. He realised it was an important message; it was also important that he do well with it. In the event, despite his initial dismay, and with the aid of a dictionary, he made a satisfactory job of it and John Gennings was pleased. It had been a test of Hugh's ability, a near thing, but Hugh came through.

For what Gennings did for him in the early years of their association, Hugh was always grateful. From the first the older man took an interest in the younger, training him for greater things, preparing him, in fact, for the succession, as Hugh later interpreted it. And in the process of learning from the expert Hugh was acquiring a skill with words which was to be invaluable to him years afterwards when he was engaged in writing and preaching.

Under the tutelage of John Gennings, Hugh learned how to write to an absolute minimum of words in order to save money in the sending of telegrams. He claimed that that training was invaluable when he came to write a weekly newspaper 'sermon', which had a limit of a hundred words, including the text. Those 'One-minute Sermons' were widely-read and brought incalculable blessing to countless numbers of people around the world. Asked over and over again how he managed to put so much into so little space, Hugh said this was one of the things for which John Gennings had unwittingly prepared him.

He was also well-trained by Gennings in the reverse process, learning how to clothe the incoming telegrams 'with flesh'. He became proficient at filling out the barest outline into a lively coherent story. Gennings was himself a master at this, and would defend himself vigorously against any critic who accused him of writing into a brief message more than was intended. He claimed he never invented or misrepresented.

Hugh also acquired the art, whilst modestly denying he ever reached the heights of his mentor. Such skill as he did acquire, however, he claimed helped him immeasurably in later years. He said he knew of few things more stimulating than to take a section of Scripture and do with it what he had years before learned to do with those incoming telegrams: to discover the mind of the original writer and build up the background. That Hugh became an excellent preacher, with an ability to hold large audiences fascinated, and then to present them with the challenge of Christ, will be agreed by all who were privileged to hear him.

Here is a brief extract from a sermon on the woman of Samaria, with the title 'Instant Harvest', and the text: 'The woman then left her water-pot' (John 4: 28):

The scene then is the well sunk by the patriarch Jacob near the foot of Mount Gerizim, the sacred mountain of the Samaritans. It is a day in May, and the time is high noon, the hottest hour. The well is a natural hiding place for travellers on the Great North Road which connects Jerusalem with the Mediterranean at Acre. And up that road there comes a party of men: Jesus of Nazareth and some of His earliest followers. . . . (The woman's) response is probably just what He wanted and expected. She is highly sceptical. How and where is He going to get this water He speaks of? Somebody greater than Jacob, the giver of the well. The water was good enough for him.

I shall make bold to say that, at this, a twinkle of inner knowledge came into the Master's eye . . . I do believe that Christ had a smile which pierced the armour of many a sinner. I catch a glimpse of it, over the rim of the cup from which He sips gratefully. 'Thank you,' He says, 'That's lovely! It won't cure a thirst though. It will only relieve it. But the water that I can offer to people is all the water they'll ever want — a constant spring within themselves.' He knew the woman needed this 'water'.

Who could doubt that through John Gennings God was preparing Hugh Redwood for his great future work as a religious writer and preacher?

*   *   *

Important writing assignments came Hugh's way during his years with Central News. These included the reporting of the funeral service for King Edward the Seventh in St. George's Chapel Windsor — an experience he valued enormously. Incidentally, seated either side of him in the organ loft where, with other reporters, he was given his place, were two men who became famous in the world of literature: Edgar Wallace and Philip Gibbs.

Hugh was also 'in', from the reporting angle, on the coronation of King George the Fifth, the sinking of the *Titanic*, the death and funeral of William Booth, Founder and first General of The Salvation Army, and other great events. But the biggest story he was ever called upon to handle, he said, was the tragic yet glorious expedition of Scott to the South Pole.

Central News made careful arrangements to act as Scott's agent — for receiving and transmitting the story to the world. They planned to send a man from London to meet Scott's ship, the *Terra Nova*, when it reached New Zealand at the conclusion of the expedition, which, it was anticipated, would be in the spring of 1912. It is now history that the expedition went wrong and that Scott did not return to New Zealand. When the facts of the disaster came out it was Hugh Redwood who received the story, sitting for two days and nights while it came in section by section. He wrote later that he typed his manuscript, at times, with tears coursing down his face. He tried to read some of it aloud to his office colleagues but choked in the attempt. Apart from the man who was transmitting the story, and the cable operators who were handling it, he was the first to read it. He concluded his account of his involvement with this momentous event with the words: 'Let us thank God for men like Scott whose deeds live on to show us the way of endeavour.'

During these years he was privileged, in the course of his reporting duties, to come up close to many of the leading figures of the day: Asquith, Balfour, Winston Churchill, Lloyd George. Possessing the eye and ear of the thoroughly professional journalist, he made his own estimation of such men. He rated Churchill much lower than Asquith and Balfour as a speaker, and expressed his opinion that few could have imagined in those days to what oratorical heights Churchill would rise. Lloyd George he rated very highly indeed. His words, he said, were set to music, so that in reporting him he nearly fell down on the job — he wanted to listen all the time and with his

whole attention, and risked neglecting to make the essential
notes. He once listened to the great Welshman delivering one
address in his native tongue and though he could not understand a syllable of it, it was not long before he felt sure he
agreed with him!

*   *   *

Hugh did not serve in the military forces during the First
World War. An injury to his left eye, occasioned when, as a
four-year-old, he fell downstairs, resulted in a permanent
squint. So when, in 1915, he volunteered for Lord Derby's
Army, he was rejected. Three years later he was summoned for
a medical examination along with thousands of older men (he
was then thirty-five) but he was again declared unfit. He spent
the whole of the war in London at his own job, except for six
months when, on the doctor's advice, he worked on a Somerset
farm.

There was now the reporting of war news, the novel experience of working within the bounds of censorship, the coping
with the extra demands necessitated by a diminished staff, and
the equally novel but far more frightening experience of air
raids. Though he said, referring no doubt to his rejection for
military service, that the war passed him by, it did further
harden his heart against religion. The carnage, the destruction,
the whole tragic business affected him deeply. If there was a
God, why did He not do something about it? he asked over and
over again. He told himself that he had no faith; such as he had
once possessed was now dead. It was not true, of course. Faith
was depressed, but not utterly extinguished. The day was
coming when it would flourish again.

In an unhappy incident with John Gennings which resulted

in Hugh's dismissal from Central News, the fault was possibly equally divided. In his account of the affair Hugh made no suggestion that this was so: John Gennings was in the wrong! But Hugh could be touchy, quick to take offence, especially in the days before his conversion.

It happened like this. Six months' leave of absence was advised by a medical specialist who told Hugh he should get away from London and live an open-air life for some time (he took a farm-labourer's job in Somerset). Hugh returned to an embarrassing situation. He was told by Gennings, in writing, that in future Hugh and his night staff — two other men — would have to cover emergency news themselves. In the event of anything 'breaking' during the night the sub-editors would have to collect the news and then handle it. No reporters were available. Hugh pointed out that the war was still on: an emergency such as the devastation following an air-raid could occur at any time. It was unreasonable to expect the subs to work like that; their normal responsibilities were heavy enough owing to reduced editorial staff. But Gennings would not budge. Hugh was hurt, especially as Gennings' communication with him in the matter was conducted in a so-formal way. Their association had hitherto always been of the most friendly kind. They had been used to talking over and deciding things together up till now. But as Hugh would not resign, Gennings curtly gave him notice.

It is not easy to understand why Hugh should have considered that in war-time conditions, with the acute shortage of man-power on the home front, Gennings' instruction was all that unreasonable. He had not realised, of course, that Gennings was a dying man. The news that he had gone came to Hugh only a few weeks after he had left the agency. In effect he admitted that, had he known Gennings was ill, his reaction would have been different. But he did claim that it could not be said that they parted bad friends.

While unsure of what to do in the dispute with Gennings, Hugh consulted both his father and a friend, H. W. Smith, who was the night editor of the *Daily News*. When it became plain that he was not going to continue his association with the agency (and both his father and Smith advised against accepting Gennings' instruction) it was Smith who was instrumental in securing him a post as sub-editor with his own paper. Hugh was delighted. He could hardly believe his good fortune. Those who worked on the *Daily News* were considered in the newspaper world of the day to be well-placed and secure.

*   *   *

Hugh began his new work on April 1, 1918. Before the end of the war he had been transferred by Smith, who was his immediate chief, from general sub-editing to the foreign news desk and it was not long before he was the paper's foreign editor. He held that important post for seven years; years he considered among the happiest of his career.

During this period he travelled extensively and met and interviewed several Heads of State and other leading figures of the day, including Chancellor Gustav Stresemann of Germany, King Alfonso of Spain and Karl Radek of Russia (in the Kremlin). He briefly described these exciting years in *God in the Shadows* (writing of himself in the third person, a device he employed throughout that book).

He roamed the whole of Europe, studied Fascism in Italy and Bolshevism in Russia, worked in Berlin where you paid for taxis in notes of a milliard marks, and saw for himself how prohibition worked in Norway and the United States. Also he saw the identical spots where Moses made the acquaintance of Pharaoh's daughter (a Coptic gentleman of mercenary instincts gave him assurances about this); where the infant Christ rested with His parents on the flight into Egypt, and where His followers by hundreds met death in the arena.

But in 1926 Henry Cadbury, who ran the *Daily News*, decided on some changes on the paper, and Hugh was made night editor. This was not a post he would have chosen for himself. He said that the appointment 'condemned' him 'to hard labour anew within the walls of an office'. He went so far as to say that had he been told earlier that he would be transferred to the night editorship, he might have left the *Daily News* for another paper where he understood there was an opening more to his taste. But later he considered that that would have been a grave mistake. Looking back he detected a design in his life, and the appointment as night editor was part of the pattern. He wrote: 'Several years ahead as yet, a new kind of work altogether awaited me, and I now see that, before I could undertake it, it was essential for me to have an intensive education possible only if my days were free and I remained in the same employment.' For Hugh, all things worked together for good.

Before examining that 'new kind of work', Christian work, we must see how the life-transforming experience occurred that made it all possible. We must also recall some of the joys and shadows of Hugh's family life.

CHAPTER 3

The Road Back

IT WAS EDITH, we recall, who was instrumental in securing Hugh's position with the Central News Agency. That was in 1905. Three years later they married and after honeymooning in Scotland, which cost Hugh all of six weeks' salary (thirty pounds), they settled in Catford, south of the Thames. Two years later their only child, a daughter, was born. Hugh's joy knew no bounds. He had wanted a daughter more than a son, a daughter who would share his own love of music, but who would outshine him by far as a musician.

During his early years in Bristol he had frequently deputised for the music critic of the *Western Daily Press*, and though he felt he wrote some reasonable reviews, he was painfully aware that in matters musical his enthusiasm considerably outweighed his knowledge.

He played the piano and organ fairly well, and had had a little choral training. He boasted late in life that he could still sing most of the psalms without a book. He loved to attend recitals, concerts and the opera — his greatest love — when he could. But that was the limit so far as musical performance and appreciation were concerned. After he came to London, of course, there was more for him to enjoy: more concerts, more orchestras, the Proms; and with Edith he made as much of all these as his slender means would allow.

His daughter, however, would be given the finest musical education he could secure for her. She would have the best teachers, study on the continent; and he dreamed of the day when she would give public recitals of her own compositions.

Gwen did become a fine musician, though a cruel blow to her health just as she was blossoming into young womanhood was to limit the range of her accomplishments. When the inexplicable happened, so suddenly, so unexpectedly, Hugh was devastated. But a shattering experience of a very different kind preceded it. For the second time Hugh was converted.

*   *   *

Hugh's first encounter with The Salvation Army was of short duration, as we have seen. Little over twelve months after he had knelt at the Penitent-form at Bristol Citadel Corps he was doing his best to forget. Soon he was drinking and smoking again, and before long had 'thrown in his lot' — as he put it — with a company of people who 'fancied themselves Bohemian', and who delighted to scandalise the neighbourhood with their fun and frolics. Hugh entered into their escapades with as much enthusiasm as the best — or the worst — of them.

Yet, looking back on those undisciplined days, he recalled occasions when he was unexpectedly brought up against Salvationists. He never seemed to be able entirely to get away from them. And that meant that he could not get away from God. He said that there were things that happened to him from time to time which made him feel as if other eyes were watching him. He was being pursued. As with Francis Thompson, the Hound of Heaven would not let him go.

On one occasion, not long after his 'defection', he heard the sound of a hymn being sung in the open air by a group of Salvationists some distance away, hidden from his sight. He was homeward bound after a 'more or less discreditable escapade' and the singing 'stirred a revolt at his mode of living and wakened a wish at his heart'. The Salvationists sang:

> Thou would'st be saved,
> Why not tonight?

and the words, he felt, were directed at him.

Even when he visited the police courts on reporting assignments he found that the Army was always there, in the person of a woman-officer who was on duty in case anyone brought before the magistrates needed her help. The officer knew that Hugh had once 'belonged', and she frequently sent reproachful looks his way. Or so Hugh thought. It may have been his imagination, of course: his conscience troubling him. But he felt uncomfortable in her presence.

After he arrived in London, however, he settled down. He was no longer the 'Bohemian' youth conducting himself in the outrageous manner of earlier days. Soon he was a married man who went to church regularly with his wife. This did not mean that there was anything even remotely resembling a personal commitment to Christ. In fact, despite the churchgoing, he had serious doubts about, and no desire for, the Christian faith. Nevertheless, it seemed to him, the Pursuer continued to pursue.

Hugh was among the thousands of people who, in August 1912, went to pay their last respects to William Booth, Founder and first General of The Salvation Army, at the lying-in-state at the Clapton Congress Hall. In a strange way Hugh still considered him 'his' General. A song sung then by a group of girl-cadets had an extraordinary effect upon him. They sang the very song the Bristol Salvationists had sung years before when he knelt at the Penitent-form:

> For you I am praying,
> I'm praying for you.

Was this, like the song in the open air, just a coincidence? he asked himself. He began to doubt it.

Had it been also a coincidence that the Salvationist publicity officer he had met earlier, in the course of reporting the old General's illness, was a Bristolian also, a friendly man he came to like and respect?

There was yet another incident which Hugh put on record and about which he asked himself once more: Was it only co-incidence? Late one night, not long after the visit to the Clapton Congress Hall which had affected him so deeply, three men-officers of The Salvation Army called at his house. They were in London for the General's funeral and had been directed to a billet in the Catford area but had missed their way. Seeing a light in Hugh's window they called to ask for directions. Hugh was glad to advise them, but as he put them on the right path he mused again, not without wonder, on the regularity, the *uncomfortable* regularity, with which he had lately come into contact with The Salvation Army – with the messengers of God?

He found himself growing increasingly disturbed, and not a little irritated, when he encountered Salvation Army officers in Queen Victoria Street where the Army's Headquarters were situated, only a stone's throw from Fleet Street where he himself had his office.

But imagine his amazement when, one day, on a poster in the High Street where he lived, he saw the name of an officer he had known years before in Bristol. It was the very man with whom he could not see eye to eye and from whom, so soon after his conversion, he had parted company, to go back to his old (and worse) ways. He looked at the name on the poster and wished these Army people would leave him alone!

He did find the grace, however, to visit the officer — who had been appointed to the district — and the breach between them was healed, so much so, that Hugh made a visit to a Salvation Army hall and, in fact, said a word from the platform. That was at Camberwell. But it was a once-only occasion. Years were to pass before he was to enter an Army building again.

*   *   *

It was only much later that Hugh was able to make the surrender that was to turn his world upside down.

This happened in the spring of 1927. Hugh was in his study at home listening to a broadcast service from Holy Trinity Church in Folkestone. He had been interested in wireless since the day when a colleague had presented him with one of extreme simple design, contained in a cigar box. So it was not as a worshipper, but as a radio fan, that he tuned in that evening. But what he heard from the preacher, the Rev. W. H. Elliott, stopped him in his tracks.

The preacher was talking about prayer, and one statement fastened itself on Hugh's mind: 'Nobody knows what he may be doing if he prays for a friend tonight.' Was someone praying for *him*? Were the prayers of Salvationists who, perhaps, had never ceased to have faith for him being effective even at this moment? ('For you I am praying, I'm praying for you,' the cadets sang, years before at Clapton, he remembered.)

Certain it is that as the preacher's words came to Hugh, he became conscious again of that irresistible influence he had felt through the years in those strange, unlooked-for encounters with the Salvationists. And the voice that spoke to him was, he knew, the Voice which, twenty-six years before, had made itself heard between the lines of the address by Mrs. Bramwell Booth in the Broadmead Baptist Church in Bristol.

He described his feelings in *God in the Shadows*:

(The influence) was greater than anything he had known; more urgent; more definite; an immense longing, and side by side with it, an immense self-revelation. He was taken completely by surprise: he had no time to fight against it; he saw himself and was ashamed. The secrets of his selfish life were dragged to light, and they bowed him down till he ached with the burden of them. And all at once he knew that a Hand was held out to him, that here, undreamed of, unexplained, was God, and a chance of heaven.

He did not hesitate. He did not doubt it: it was too real for doubt. The service was over: he rose from his chair and went up to his bedroom. There at his bedside, with a child's trust, he took the Hand that was offered to him and, devoid of faith as he was, prayed that faith might be given him. He knew that his prayer was heard, for an extraordinary sense of lightness came to him; he felt a buoyancy, a gladness, a singing at the heart.

Hugh was converted. The thrill of it was to remain with him for the rest of his long and busy life. It was to affect, in ways undreamed of at the beginning, all that he subsequently would do.

* * *

Answering the question, 'Why do you believe in conversion?' Hugh once said: 'My belief in conversion is based on the unassailable truth that God has converted me. I am a changed man, leading a changed life.'

For the rest of his days he was to preach not only the possibility but the necessity of conversion. The words of Jesus, 'Ye must be born again', were at the centre of his far-reaching ministry. He saw a good deal of formal conventional religion; religion as a habit, that had affected no dynamic transformation of the life. Indeed, this had been his own kind of religion for years. Not until he had a personal experience of conversion did he understand what God really intended for His children.

He tasted the wonder of this, first of all, as we have seen, when, as an eighteen-year-old, he knelt at the Penitent-form at Bristol Citadel. His subsequent backsliding did not, he averred, mean that that was not a genuine conversion.

'I have Christian friends', he said, 'who hold that, having been "saved", I could not therefore be "lost", and *that* I do not believe, for only too well I know that, after a year of Salvation Army membership, followed by a quarter of a century in the wilderness, I was more truly lost than ever before.'

One of the eleven points of Salvation Army doctrine says

that 'We believe that continuance in a state of salvation depends upon continual obedient faith in Christ', and though, following his conversion in 1927 Hugh Redwood did not for the second time become a Salvationist, preferring to retain his membership with the Anglican Church while being closely associated with, and working assiduously for the Army, he wholeheartedly subscribed to that article of faith. Following his own experience, how could he do otherwise?

For Hugh, conversion meant that the past was forgiven, that he had been saved from death and sin, and also that a glorious new life had begun. It meant, to use his own words, both 'rescue' and 'purpose'. It was a simple uncomplicated faith, for Hugh had a simple uncomplicated theology. It was the theology of the Salvationists with whom he was to find both enriching fellowship and ever-expanding channels of service. The 'S's' on their uniform speak that basic message: 'Saved to Serve'.

*   *   *

Central to the experience of conversion, as Hugh found it, was total joy in Christ. He felt this at the point of encounter on both occasions — when he was eighteen and twenty-six years later. On the earlier occasion he wrote of having gained, not 'a sense of ecstasy, no sudden irradiation', but an exhilarating sense of liberty that 'filled his lungs like the Mendip wind and spread broad landscapes before him'. Joy, deep joy!

Of the second encounter with Christ he wrote: 'Dear God, the wonder of it, the loving wonder of it!' Joy, deep joy! This time it was to remain, because the experience remained. There was no second backsliding. He was older now, and wiser. The forty-four-year-old was not so susceptible to the influences that affected the eighteen-year-old. The disapproval of parents, the fear of the taunts of his work-a-day colleagues when, with cap and jersey, he identified with the members of The Salvation Army in Bristol Citadel Corps, many of them of extremely humble origin; to say nothing of the temptations that came when as a new, promising, out-of-the-usual convert, he was thrust so quickly into the limelight — all affected the boy and led to his backsliding.

But it was different with the man ... it was easier, though not always *easy*. He was more readily 'able to stand against the wiles of the devil' (Ephesians 6: 11) and win through to a glorious future. And, though not without some 'ups and downs' it was essentially joy, joy all the way. Hugh wrote:

There is (no romance) so glorious as the romance of conversion. For it takes the drabbest and dreariest life and makes it a thing of glowing colour. It takes the lowliest life and illumines it with friendship. It gives purpose to the daily round, direction to the common task and to both a place of importance in God's great scheme.

We shall see later that Bible study and prayer figured prominently in his life and were precious to him, and also that he believed in the necessity for the soul to be entirely surrendered to God. Now, however, we must consider that other life-shaking experience that came to him; this time a dark, frightening thing. Its shadow was already gathering round him as he sat in his study listening to the voice of God through the voice of the broadcasting preacher. But the light that came as he made his response was so real, so strengthening that the darkness could not overcome it.

CHAPTER 4

Through the Shadows

FEW MEN GO through life knowing nothing of human suffering in one form or another, and Hugh Redwood was not among them. But he came triumphantly through, though not easily and not before agonising doubts had stormed his mind and all but broken his heart.

Writing in the years of his Christian maturity about human suffering (*God in the Everyday*) Hugh affirmed his faith that, though evil must be accepted as an active spiritual force, intelligently controlled, and though much will always remain that is inexplicable, out of it all God can produce good and thus triumph. To show the truth of this he records story after story from his knowledge of experiences through which other people passed, but the greatest proof of all to him was in what happened in his own home, and, we shall see later, in his own body.

Hugh's daughter, Gwen, was sixteen at the time of his conversion. She had done well with her studies and, in particular, had developed her gift for music. Her father's hopes for her in this area were being realised, and there was more to follow.

Hugh was proud. The ambitions he had cherished for her since the day of her birth had never left him. He considered no sacrifice too great to make for her.

Gwen herself recalls one outstanding example. When she was in her early teens and her father was foreign editor of the *Daily News*, he was offered a position abroad, in Calcutta, which carried promotion and a much higher salary. Hugh turned down the job as being too great a health hazard on account of the unfavourable climatic conditions in that part of the world. It was not himself that he had in mind when he declined the promotion, but his wife and daughter, who in the event of his acceptance would have had to share the inconveniences with him. And, of course, Gwen's education would have been affected and nothing must be allowed to interfere with that.

*   *   *

As Gwen approached her seventeenth birthday, to be celebrated in May, and also the termination of her schooldays at the end of the summer term, a family cruising holiday was planned for August which would take them to Norway. Though berths were booked, the holiday never took place. In the middle of June Gwen arrived home from a visit to a friend in a state of collapse. At first this was thought by her mother to be nothing more than end-of-term fatigue; a little rest would put her right.

The next day, however, which was Sunday, the symptoms showed no signs of disappearing and the doctor was called. He did not think there was anything seriously wrong and prescribed for influenza and said that, as a precaution, he would call again next morning. There was no cause for alarm. Both

Hugh and Edith were reassured and on Monday Hugh went as usual to the office. But he was quickly summoned home again and arrived white-faced and shaken. He had not been given all the details over the telephone but what had been said was sufficient to tell him that things were serious. Meeting him in the hall, Edith put her arms around him. 'Gwen is gravely ill,' she said, her face showing shock and bewilderment. 'There are signs of paralysis.'

Later Hugh recorded his reaction to the frightening news:

Oh, no, that couldn't be true ... She had never known what it was to be ill. A cold, perhaps, and measles when she was a baby, but nothing to cause an instant's fear. And now this deadly, ghastly fear that was rising as numbness passed. Oh, God, if she were to die! Perhaps she was dying. Dying? He must be mad to think of such a thing. But he looked again in his wife's eyes and saw what was written there ... (*God in the Shadows*)

He knew he had to take a grip on himself, and then he remembered. Six weeks before he had re-discovered his faith in God. He could not have prayed, really prayed, before that. Now he could, now he must, now he would. It was not easy at first. He could not frame a prayer, his own prayer that is, and even when he fell back on the familiar Lord's prayer, he stumbled and then stopped at 'Thy will be done'. How could *this* be the will of God who but six weeks before had come to him in love and assurance as he sat in his study and listened to the message of the broadcasting preacher?

It was not much of a prayer. There was not a great deal of faith in it. Yet prayer it was and faith of a kind; he had said,

and had said from his heart: 'Our *Father* . . .' And had not
Jesus said something about the one who had faith as a grain of
mustard seed, the smallest of seeds, saying to a mountain,
remove to another place and it should remove? (Matthew
17:20).

The next few days were agony. Death was never far away.
Tuesday came, and there was no improvement at all that morning, and only a little at night. But the next day the fever
heightened and, answering Hugh's question: 'How is she?' the
doctor had to say: 'I wish I had better news for you! but it is
my duty to tell you she is markedly worse.'

After receiving that devastating word, Hugh went to say
good night to his wife who, exhausted, was preparing to take a
few hours' rest, reluctant though she was to leave her daughter's
bedside. But there could be no real rest for Hugh. He was
fighting the greatest battle of his life and he had to win
through. He went into the study where God had so recently
revealed Himself, and knelt by a chair and again tried to pray.
This time, as he bowed in the presence of omnipotent love and
poured out at last his feeble words, his heart went out in
confident trust. 'It was', he said, 'as if a great Specialist had
arrived, and I was laying the case before him.' And he knew, in
that moment of prayer, that despite appearances, despite all the
doctor had said, Gwen would not die.

His feeling was confirmed when he rose from his knees,
picked up a copy of Weymouth's New Testament lying on a
nearby table and took to himself, as a word from God for that
dark hour, the first verse his eyes lighted upon: 'We have therefore a cheerful confidence (2 Corinthians 5: 6).

It is not likely that Hugh's regular idea of seeking guidance
from God was to pick a text at random and accept that as divine

light in a particular situation. As Hugh developed in Christian discipleship he would see, like any mature believer, the potential dangers in such a procedure. He believed that God's word reveals its treasures and its message to those who study and search to a plan and programme. But there are exceptions to the most time-tested rule, and in that moment, for that situation of need, he took the word from Weymouth's as God's sign. He believed God was saying to him: 'Hugh, your prayer is answered. Your daughter is not going to die!'

He placed on record the indisputable fact that at the time he was on his knees in prayer the fever left Gwen. In that very hour her temperature fell dramatically from 104.6 to 99 degrees and stayed at that point for the rest of the night. The temperature chart kept at the foot of the bed and marked regularly by the duty nurse showed that this was so. There it was, the inked line falling steeply away to hold steady at the point that marked the beginning of hope. Hugh had experienced his second miracle. His daughter would live!

* * *

Gwen never again completely recovered her health. Never again was she fully mobile. All her father's long-held hopes for her were not to be realised. This was part of the mystery of life, of suffering, that Hugh did not pretend to be able to fathom. He confessed as much, though he also said that one day he *would* know. He was content to leave it there. Though he may not have sung it, Hugh believed the words of the old hymn:

> Not now, but in the coming years,
> It may be in the better land,
> We'll read the meaning of our tears,
> And there, sometime, we'll understand.

Gwen was able to bring enrichment to many as the years sped by, not only through her music — though her accomplishment in this was not small. She fulfilled a prophecy Hugh made about her as the days unfolded, that in some way she too was part of the great plan, and that she would be 'linked with the lives of multitudes'.

Hugh told Gwen's story in *God in the Shadows*, and miracles followed, miracles wrought in the lives of many who read and responded to the message of hope in those pages. In that way her father's prophecy came true.

When she was well enough to be moved, Gwen was admitted to Charing Cross Hospital. She was there for eight long months, and the day of her discharge did not spell the end of her troubles. Hopes were raised and then overthrown; disappointment followed disappointment, recovery, such as it was, was slow indeed. It was hard for the three of them, and Hugh, convinced of God's care though he was, sometimes asked the question why?

However, this direct contact with suffering gave him something he could have received in no other way.

He was able to visit Gwen during the day time, for her transfer to the hospital coincided with his own transfer from the chair of foreign editor of his paper to that of night editor. His days were now free. On his frequent visits to his daughter, he glimpsed at first hand, not only in her but also in others, the qualities that suffering can reveal. He was, he said, 'braced' by his contact with it. And he found in his involvement with others' needs the joy and a sense of satisfaction that can come to a human being from outgoing service to others as from no other activity.

He particularly enjoyed the efforts he made to brighten the

lives of the children, for their ward was on the same floor as
Gwen's. At Christmas he was Santa Claus, and that he made a
huge success of it should not be doubted because he said so
himself when he described his adventure in this regard!

He was being transformed. He saw, looking back, that even
this dark experience was being woven by the Divine Designer
into a plan. The 'why?' came back now and again, but he was
beginning to see how all of human experience could be used in
the life of the trusting soul to further God's purpose among
men. It *was* true — even out of inexplicable suffering, God
could bring good.

*   *   *

About this time Hugh began to attend Salvation Army meetings again. One evening, when Edith was at the hospital with
Gwen, he entered the Catford hall where a small group of
people had gathered for a meeting. When the invitation was
given for anyone present to testify to the grace and goodness of
God, Hugh rose to his feet and spoke.

Unfortunately he left no record of what he said. It cannot
have been easy to say anything at all. It was no fewer than
twenty-six years since he had made that initial contact with
the Army at Bristol, knelt at the Penitent-form and donned,
and quickly doffed, the uniform; he had not been in an Army
hall for some time, only once in fact, at Camberwell, in many
years. And at Catford he was a stranger.

But, on the other hand, he had recently re-discovered his
faith, and the thrill of that life-transforming experience with
the risen Christ was still upon him: he never lost it. Furthermore, God had been so wonderfully good. Gwen was still very
poorly; it was unlikely that she would walk again, but she *was*

alive. He had prayed with tears that she would not die, and God had heard.

So, while we are the poorer for not knowing exactly what Hugh said when he got to his feet in that Catford meeting, praise to God must have been central to his words. How could it have been otherwise?

Rebellious feelings over what had recently happened to him and his loved ones had all but disappeared. He said as much in his own record of these events. Before many weeks, and many more visits to the Army, had passed, including one to the Regent Hall, the Army's famous centre in the West End of London, which included taking part in a march with Salvationists through theatre land, his rebellion had gone for ever.

Thus it was that Hugh Redwood came back. Before the bells had rung in the New Year, 1928, he was completely God's man again. The divine plan, a plan that had required so many strange and diverse elements for its outworking, was about to reach its greatest stage. God had remarkable things in store for His servant, and His servant was ready.

CHAPTER 5

Getting Involved

ROMANTICISED STORIES ABOUT the lives and experiences of notable people which bear little relation to the facts often gain currency after their deaths, but so far as Hugh Redwood was concerned this happened while he was very much alive. He said that on many occasions, in the course of being introduced as a speaker, he had to listen while the audience was treated to quite erroneous accounts of how he came into contact with The Salvation Army, and started his work for the Kingdom of God.

He was *not* sent as a reporter of the *Daily News* to investigate and write an account of the Westminster floods disaster of 1928. He was the night editor who had nothing directly to do with the initial reports that appeared as a 'scoop' in his newspaper. And he was *not* converted there and then in the Westminster streets as a result of the impression made upon him by the self-sacrificing endeavours of Salvationists who toiled in Christ's name on behalf of the victims of the disaster.

He was certainly impressed by what he saw when he visited the unhappy area, so impressed, indeed, that from there he was led into extraordinary avenues of service for God and humanity. But he was converted some months before 'Westminister', as he sat in his own room listening to a broadcasting preacher. And following that life-changing experience he had linked up, if somewhat loosely with the Salvation Army corps at Catford where he lived.

But long before that, as an eighteen-year-old, he had been a member of The Salvation Army in Bristol and had even worn the peaked cap and the scarlet, crested jersey for a time.

All this we have seen. May the mistaken accounts which irritated Hugh so much, and which even now are sometimes recounted in one form or another, disappear for ever!

* * *

When Hugh travelled to Westminster on the day following the floods disaster of 1928, the work of rescue was in full swing. He went along on an impulse, which he later recognised and acknowledged as divine guidance, to see what he could do to help. He knew from later editions of his paper that Salvationists were deeply involved in the work being carried out for the victims, and he looked them out.

We have already noted how the women-officers of the Army's Slum Department gladly accepted his offer of help and invited him to share their labours. Perhaps it ought to be recorded here — in these days of 'women's liberation' — that Hugh first approached a group of *men*-Salvationists, but they told him they were managing quite well, thank you!

That initial contact with his 'sisters of the slums' — as he later named them — was to start him on a far-reaching mission for God that was to touch countless lives and immeasurably enrich his own. It was the utter dedication of those gentle, godly women to the service of the poor and most degraded, he said, that impressed him.

There was one particular incident that reached his heart as did nothing else that he witnessed and shared on that memorable afternoon.

The officers were trying to find accommodation for the night for an old couple who had lost their home and all their pitifully few worldly goods. The old people were wet, hungry and unbelievably dirty. Captain Lucy Warren, who had grown up in lovely Somerset, an area as far removed in character from the grime and confusion of that Westminster scene as any place could be, said to her assistant, without any affectation: 'They can have our beds, Lieutenant, I expect we shall be here all night!' Hugh wrote later, 'From that minute I felt sure that these women were working for and with Christ.'

Such dedication challenged him strongly. What was *he*, Hugh Redwood, willing to do and give on behalf of others? Was *he* as ready to follow Christ into difficult and uncongenial paths of service as were these devoted women of the slums?

The questions disturbed him; they demanded an answer and he knew the answer must come through prayer. So he made his prayer. It was simply: 'Lord, lead me, and I will follow step by step.' And when, much later, he looked back upon his long life of service he knew that prayer had been answered. God did mark out a path for his feet and he walked in it humbly and gratefully.

*　　　*　　　*

Not long after the events of Westminster Hugh went to Brighton for a short holiday. While he was there he attended a meeting at the Congress Hall Corps of The Salvation Army.

The officer preached on the text: 'Launch out into the deep' (Luke 5:4), and emphasised the fact that Jesus spoke those words from a 'dirty, smelling fishing boat'. He did not withhold Himself from the unpleasant, even sordid things of life, the preacher went on, and nor should we. No task is too ordinary and menial for the servants of One who was born in the out-house of a little country inn and who moved among the sick, poor and deprived spreading hope and joy. The officer was Adjutant (later Colonel) Arthur Knapman, and Hugh always acknowledged that he owed him a great deal. Years later he wrote to him, enclosing an autographed copy of *Bristol Fashion*. 'Maybe it would never have been written but for you — who can say?' he said. 'I am perfectly sure that that Saturday night talk of yours at Brighton Congress Hall away back in 1928 was one of the major factors in the decisions I was called upon to make, and sometimes the mere thought of all I should have missed had I not "launched out" makes me feel like coming out in a perspiration.' And he signed the book: 'With affectionate regards', quoting the Scripture upon which the Brighton sermon was based.

As he listened to the Adjutant's talk Hugh knew he was receiving a call from God. This was confirmed when a little later he visited Brighton again and was taken to a slum post in the town by a Salvationist, one Bob Green, who in everyday life was a greengrocer and who had befriended Hugh on his first visit. Hugh had never imagined that the lovely seaside town would have the need of Slum Posts, but he was learning fast. He went to an open-air meeting led by the Slum officers and was drawn to the people who gathered around to listen to the Army, especially to the children. In true Army style they had been taught a chorus and he said it was their singing, and the actions they had been encouraged to make as a lively accompaniment, that did it. He knew in that moment that the children of the mean streets were to be his children. He knew that with them, and with all who lived in the slums, he had to get involved.

A thoroughly professional newspaper man, well used to moving decisively when a move was indicated, Hugh immediately wrote to Major Mary Patch, the lady he had seen in action at Westminister on the afternoon following the floods, and whose work he had observed with admiration, but it was in fact to Lieutenant-Colonel Edith Colbourne, the Head of the Slum Department, that, after some delay, he was eventually directed. Her advice to him was not: 'Come and join us', which may seem strange, especially to a Salvationist. It is not difficult to see how that could well have been her message. The Army is always looking for those who, motivated by love to God and man, will swell its ranks, put themselves 'under orders' and engage wholeheartedly (and especially full time) in the cause for which Salvationists believe the Movement was raised up. It is not every day that a highly successful journalist at the top of his profession offers his services to the Army.

But Lieutenant-Colonel Colbourne counselled him not to become a Salvationist unless he was absolutely sure that it was God's will for him. And he was not absolutely sure at that moment or he would hardly have been seeking advice. She said: 'God may have other plans for you, bigger plans maybe; this Army contact is only a beginning.'

How wise! And how different a reaction from that of the Salvationists of Bristol nearly thirty years before who pressed him too quickly and too soon into all kinds of activities.

Around this time he also had a talk with a young Slum

officer, Captain Eva Pankhurst, now Mrs. Lieutenant-Colonel Jewkes, who lives in retirement in South London. She spoke to Hugh of her own call to service and lent him a copy of Henry Drummond's *The Greatest Thing in the World*. Together, Hugh said, these women gave him an entirely new outlook. He saw clearly now that, to use his own words, 'to sacrifice my calling was not necessarily to abandon it'. So he resolved not to give up his journalism but rather give it to God, to sacrifice it on the altar of divine service. It need not be a case of journalist *or* evangelist, but both. If God was wanting him to bring them together, should he seek to put them asunder? So journalist *and* evangelist it was to be from that day forward. How it was to work out in practice he could not then know, but time was to prove how right a decision he made.

*   *   *

Hugh remained a member of the Church of England to the end of his days, though his association with the Army was always very close. He would often humorously describe himself as a practising Anglo-Salvationist. His 'uniform' was an outsize silver Army shield presented to him by one of his Slum officer friends, and he wore it with pride.

From then on Hugh devoted the best part of one day a week to any task Lieutenant-Colonel Colbourne could find for him. As night editor he did not have to be at his office until four-thirty in the afternoon. This meant that from nine o'clock in the morning until his own work began he could be at the disposal of the department. Soon his officer-friends were calling him 'Brother', which suited him well.

He was given tasks which brought him a deep sense of satisfaction and which were of absorbing interest. He entered a new and demanding world. He gained, he said, an experience, social and spiritual, for which he could never be thankful enough. All this involvement in the harsh problems of the slum-dwellers was greatly appreciated by the officers with whom he worked, as well as by the people to whom he ministered. The officers who allowed him to share their labours felt privileged that he should be so ready to give his life and energy in that way. It was not only that an extra pair of hands was always appreciated, though Hugh would readily give practical help in any situation. It was something else: a kind of boost to their morale that came because someone from 'the outside', as it were, someone of Hugh's calibre, was interested in not simply sending a donation to help the work along (many excellent people supported in that way, and it was all very fine) but was willing to give himself. That was it: he gave himself; he was down there, in the grime and heartache with them.

They quickly learned to value him as a true man of God who would not hesitate to roll up his sleeves and help with the most menial task, and in the slums of those days that word *menial* covered a variety of activities from shaving a bed-ridden old man to gathering up a few cracked dishes from the table of a humble slum dwelling and washing them in a chipped enamel bowl in an antiquated outside sink. If there was coal to carry or wood to chop for a disabled old person he would do it; he would go to the shops, or smooth a pillow for a sick person. He visited homes where all kinds of needs were evident on every hand.

One who knew him well speaks of his great sympathy with the poor, but there was no patronising air about him. That would have been quickly discerned by those proud people and they would just as quickly have rejected him.

His sympathy was born of a genuine love and a desire to

share. It was the *compassion* of which the New Testament speaks, that compassion of Jesus that, literally, 'suffers with'.

He could communicate with the poor. They trusted him and were ready to share their problems with him, and they were not always, or chiefly, problems whose solutions had to be met in financial or material terms, though there were enough of these, of course, and Hugh often met them by dipping into his own slender resources. But he was always willing to help find some answer, whatever sort the need might require.

A visit he made to the Custom House Slum Post one day is recalled by Colonel Annie Connolly, who, upon her retirement some years ago, was the Secretary of the National Goodwill Department. (The term 'slum' was dropped in 1949.)

Colonel Connolly, then a young Captain, took him to see the Jones family. (That was not in fact their name, but it will serve for the purpose of the story.) Father was sick and unable to work. Mother was nearly demented by the strain of caring for six children, the youngest in the pram suffering from measles — and her financial resources were, to put it mildly, far from adequate. Those were the days of almost fifty years ago when State-provided social amenities were not nearly so plentiful as today. Poverty such as is rarely seen now was the background to the lives of countless families.

The Jones' home was pitifully poor, and neglected, but it would be unjust to lay all the blame on the sad, struggling man and wife; who could blame them if they had almost given up hope? Hugh seated himself on a backless stool in the dirty, shabby room. 'Mrs. Jones, I am not going to ask: "Is there anything you need?" It is quite obvious you need a great deal. But what do you need *most*?'

The woman directed her sad eyes towards the bare feet of

her children, pathetic little scraps of humanity who were standing around gazing uncomprehendingly at the gentleman and the Salvation Army lady in their midst. 'Shoes,' she said, 'the children have no shoes.'

'You shall have shoes for them all in a few days,' Hugh said, his words being not only words of assurance for a greatly troubled mother, but also a faith-charged prayer to a greatly caring heavenly Father.

Some would call it coincidence, Hugh called it God's loving response to a human need, but very soon, within a day or so, a letter came for Hugh and the writer enclosed ten pounds to 'be used to help someone in need'. Hugh's promise to the woman was fulfilled. The Jones' children had never worn new shoes before.

Similar incidents occurred again and again so that many people blessed him. And the officers who pointed out the needs and shared his toil, marvelled at his faith.

*   *   *

Though Hugh gave much to the slums, he learned and received much also. 'I cannot recite my debt to the Slum officers,' he wrote, 'but they taught me the meaning of prayer and the leading of Christ. He had closely observed them and he knew, as he saw them at work, that they well understood all about holiness in the common ways of life. And because of what he witnessed — and marvelled as he did so — he wrote about sanctification being not, as he had once supposed, for cloistered lives alone, but 'the property of those whose days were passed in constant touch with evil things' — a precise description of the Salvationists in whose work he had so greatly involved himself.

Those slum officers showed him, furthermore, that sanctification is as far removed from sanctimoniousness as is pole from pole; and they shared with him, he said, their serenity.

He also learned from them that sanctification is achieved only by walking the path of self-surrender. He saw his companions of the slums walking it every day of their lives. Some of them, he remembered, had come to their work in the slums from places far different in character. They had been used to walking quiet country lanes, and living in clean, fresh seaside cottages, but at Christ's call had gladly turned their back on the refinements of their accustomed ways, to labour in the squalor and grime of Britain's cities. Lovely people, some of them little more than girls, they were totally surrendered to God, willingly pledged to serve the urgent needs of their fellows.

Salvationist poet Catherine Baird wrote about one such:

> She came from sloping plains among the hills,
> Where sun had gilded fields of corn and, in
> Her youthful cheeks, still boasted of his wealth.
> Now in the sorrowing city she could hear
> The thunderings of sin and see the flash
> Of evil strike his victims till they lay
> In hideous helplessness where'er she walked . . .

*   *   *

As time went by Hugh's involvement with the slums deepened. He had found a mission, and in the conducting of it he was discovering amazing things about the ways of God with mankind. In the women he felt so privileged to work with he discerned remarkable, almost unbelievable examples of devotion to the cause of suffering humanity in the name of the One who died for all. All this moved him deeply, humbled him and strengthened his faith.

CHAPTER 6

Making Sacrifices

How were hugh's first excursions into Salvation Army service, and his new attitudes and activities received at home? Edith knew that something remarkable had happened to him and that he valued it enormously; this she accepted even if she could not share the experience with him. And she recognised that he needed the fellowship and support of vital worshipping community. What she found it difficult to understand (and Hugh admitted he felt he could not really blame her) was why he had to travel nearly two miles to the Salvation Army hall in Catford when there were churches nearer home where the methods of worship, and the people who attended, were more in keeping with that middle-class respectability to which he, and she, were accustomed and which, she believed, could well meet his needs.

When he began to give his day a week to The Salvation Army, and to make visits to Slum Posts and like centres of operations at other times as well, the atmosphere at home became more uneasy still. Daughter Gwen said, looking back on those days, that they had something like a 'divided household' for a time, and her mother found it hard.

Hugh did not absolve himself from fault in all this. He wrote later of his own 'well-intentioned blunderings' and confessed that he was 'unreasonable' in a number of ways. Though his motives were of the highest, he pursued the course on which he felt God had set his feet with insufficient regard at times for those nearest to him, two people he undoubtedly loved deeply.

In that first enthusiastic flush of his conversion experience he did not appear to pay sufficient attention to the dictum he certainly knew, that charity, in the New Testament meaning of the word, begins at home. But it was a short-lived problem, part of the growing pains of Christian maturity, to which those who knew him best, and loved him always, would readily testify.

*   *   *

Hugh felt early that full surrender to Christ involved certain 'minor sacrifices', as he called them, so he gave up smoking and became a total abstainer. There is no evidence in his writings that his associations with The Salvation Army persuaded him to take this step, though the Army is a teetotal movement, and smoking is discouraged in its members and forbidden to those who hold office in its ranks.

Hugh arrived at the decision to cut drinking and smoking right out of his life because he felt that *for him* they would be wrong. He could not, somehow, feel they were compatible with his new-found relationship with Christ. He emphasised that he did not consider this was necessarily so for every Christian, but only that he would personally have felt condemned if he had not foregone these pleasures.

His work among the slum dwellers firmly convinced him of

the misery drink could cause. Taking note of Paul's words that Christians should willingly forego that which would cause a weaker brother to stumble, even if the thing in question did little harm to the stronger, he gave up drink for ever.

He was a heavy smoker, but he prayed that his craving for tobacco be taken away in an instant, and it was. He said he never felt the desire for it again. He also said that his mind was clearer and his eye brighter as a result of these sacrifices.

Other 'minor' disciplines he exercised, he said, were in the realm of spending. He learned never to waste a penny and found he could make useful economies on such things as bus fares, walking whenever it was possible, and the coppers saved quickly mounted up, to provide extra for little kindnesses here and there.

He also resigned from his club. This, he said, was more of a sacrifice, for his club was 'one of his vanities'. He tendered his resignation 'a little sadly' though he was convinced it was one of the things he had to do. The 'sense of liberty' that possessed him once he had sent his letter away to the secretary was confirmation that he had been right to do so.

'All he had, and all he was, and all he might be' were now given up to God, he wrote, speaking of himself in the third person. The surrender was complete. And God, the persistent Pursuer, who had followed him through many years, who had never let him go, lovingly accepted his offering.

* * *

In those days, when he was in the early stages of 'working out his own salvation', his firm support, on the human level, was Elsie. She was a cousin of a friend of his; they had known each other from the Bristol days when the two families had lived in the same area of the city. Hugh considered it more than mere chance that Elsie moved to London six months before he did, and that they never lost touch through the years.

When Gwen was taken ill, Elsie was on hand to help with the nursing and was a veritable tower of strength to the whole family. Much later, when Edith died, Elsie took her place at Hugh's side; mutual deep respect and warm friendship had blossomed into love.

It was Elsie, and not Edith, who sometimes accompanied Hugh on his visits to the Slum Posts, entering into the activities with a sincerity and enthusiasm that matched his own. She had been a Sunday-school teacher for years and had also worked among poor children in London play-centres, so was very much at home with the children of the slums to whom a good deal of Hugh's 'Army' time was given.

'The children,' he wrote, 'they counted tremendously . . . There was scarcely a day of service in the slums in which they did not figure.' We have seen that Hugh believed that God used the children in the Brighton Slum Post open-air meeting to point out the direction of his future service. Small wonder then that to him they 'counted tremendously'.

Occasionally Elsie would sing solos in the meetings Hugh conducted, making her own contribution to the simple, homely form of service which, in the tradition of the Army everywhere, Hugh employed. Hugh was grateful to Elsie in those early days, as he was to be even more grateful later on. There is a wealth of feeling and meaning in the inscription he wrote in a copy of his book, *God in the Shadows*, which he presented to her. It is dated Easter, 1932, and says simply: 'To Elsie, because she understands.'

*   *   *

One day Lieutenant-Colonel Colbourne told him she had in mind the production of a pamphlet describing the work of the Slum Department and Hugh knew who had to write it. The Colonel's idea was, characteristically, a practical one. She wanted a pamphlet that would sell at a shilling (5p) to raise money for the work for which she and those who worked under her direction were responsible. It concerned her that so much of her officers' time was taken up in organising sales of work and the like to raise money. Profits from the proposed booklet would be a welcome boost to her hard-pressed funds.

This presented itself as a great challenge to Hugh. He had always wanted to write a book and had, in fact, tried his hand at a novel but (he confessed it himself) had lacked the staying power for such an enterprise. But a booklet of the kind the Colonel wanted was a different proposition. He could undertake it as a part of his service for God. What could be more satisfying? Had he not said at the beginning of his Christian adventure that he would join together journalism and evangelism?

So Hugh offered his services, and set himself to the task. What was to have been a pamphlet grew into a book, a book that became a best-seller. Hodder and Stoughton, the publishers, made a tentative agreement for 20,000 copies, but when the editor who handled the book, the Rev. Arthur Hird, read the first chapter, he said: 'Hugh, if the remaining chapters are up to the standard of this one we'll stop talking about 20,000 copies and make it a quarter of a million instead.'

God in the Slums — the title was Lieutenant-Colonel Colbourne's — ran into many editions and was translated into many languages. Even forty-five years after its writing it is still bringing inspiration and challenge to members of a generation whose knowledge of the social conditions that provide the background to that remarkable and moving volume is purely academic. Hugh devoted the whole of the royalties of *God in the Slums* to the work of The Salvation Army. They would have made him a rich man if he had kept them himself.

*　　　*　　　*

Just as he was about to begin to write *God in the Slums* Edith had a serious fall in the house and had to enter hospital for treatment and, eventually, an operation.

On her discharge the family, along with the faithful Elsie, went down to Worthing where it was hoped the change, the rest and the sea air would assist in Edith's recuperation. Then, suddenly, when they had been there only a few days, during which time Edith had shown definite signs of improvement and Hugh had made some progress on the book, he was urgently summoned back to London by his editor, Tom Clarke. At Clarke's home, away from the office where a leakage of the news could have brought panic, Hugh was told that the *Daily News* would forthwith cease to exist and would be amalgamated with the *Daily Chronicle* to form a new paper, the *News Chronicle*.

This was serious. Hundreds of men would be made redundant, for only one staff would now be needed instead of two. As a senior man, Hugh would survive, but he had the heart-breaking task of selecting thirty per cent of his own men for dismissal and, despite the fact that financial and other arrangements were made for the redundant ones, his own enforced duties in the unhappy business affected him deeply.

That was the end of the Worthing break for Hugh. He made arrangements for Edith and busied himself about the new and difficult task. On the Sunday night he brought out the first issue of the *News Chronicle*.

This newspaper was to have a life of little more than thirty years. In 1960, to the regret of many people who valued its high standards, its fairness and its excellent features, hard economics forced its closure and 3,600 employees lost their jobs. It was taken over by the *Daily Mail*. By then, of course, Hugh had retired though, as we shall see presently, a regular feature he still contributed to the paper was retained by the new owners.

However, there might be upheaval in Fleet Street but the book to which Hugh had committed himself had to be finished. Too much delay and he would have had the formidable Lieutenant-Colonel Colbourne to reckon with, a more daunting prospect even than facing his publishers! So as soon as things began to settle down a little at work he turned back to *God in the Slums*.

CHAPTER 7

A Journalist's Spotlight

OF ALL THE books Hugh wrote his first, *God in the Slums*, was without doubt the most influential. Lieutenant-Colonel Colbourne made the first approach to the publishers. Hugh had suggested that someone get in touch with the Army's Literary Department at International Headquarters so that arrangements could be made through the proper channels for publication, but the forthright Colonel said, emphatically, 'No! I'll do it myself.' So she personally contacted Hodder and Stoughton and was soon able to let Hugh know that they had accepted the idea and were ready to sign an agreement.

Hugh produced a 'book of modern miracles' as the cover said. (The Hogarth-like drawing which did so much to commend the book to the public because, as Hugh said, it was a 'striking evocation of the slums', was the work of his friend, Frank Brangwyn, who later did another drawing for Hugh's next book, *God in the Shadows*).

Hugh wrote of the slums as he saw them: of the abject poverty, the misery, the dirt and the despair. He wrote about his 'sisters of the slums', to whom the book was dedicated, who were toiling there to bring hope and brightness into sad, drab lives. He wrote not as an objective observer, rather as one who was himself deeply involved, and who counted that involvement a priceless privilege. He wrote as a servant of Him who is the ultimate answer to all human need.

The book was published in September 1930, and was an immediate success. The first printing of 20,000 copies was speedily exhausted, and ten times that number were sold in the next few months.

There was instant reaction. Even the Army itself was surprised by the story Hugh told. In an article in *The Salvation Army Year Book* for 1947 he said as much, and was gently critical of what had been the Army's attitude to the work to which he had given publicity. He considered that at the time his book was written the slum work could have done with a lot more official understanding and support, all of which it both required and deserved. He wrote:

The Salvation Army ... takes a very great deal for granted and first and foremost the grace of God. If by that grace its women were willing, nay, eager to represent Christ in the slums, and if they seemed able to make a good job of it without any male assistance, it was perfectly willing to let them do so. One consequence was that with the ceaseless growth of its other activities, it tended to take the slum work for granted, too, so that when the present writer trained a journalist's spotlight upon it in 1930, the Army in general was almost as surprised as the public at large to learn what their women were doing. Lookers-on proverbially see most of the game ...

But if, as he said, the Army was surprised at his revelations, more so were other people in the land, and, indeed, around the world. He received hundreds of letters, many of them making offers of help for the work in the slums, the result for which Lieutenant-Colonel Colbourne was hoping and for which the book had been planned.

One letter opened out a whole new area of Christian service for Hugh. It brought an invitation to preach at a Baptist Church in Walthamstow, and he had some initial hesitation in accepting. While he had conducted, and in simple terms addressed, little meetings in the Slum Posts, he knew that was quite a different matter from preaching a 'full scale' sermon at a well-attended 'middle class' church. But he did accept and began an activity that led him in the coming years into some famous pulpits in Britain and in other parts of the world.

One of his most profound memories in this connection was of speaking one Sunday afternoon at a great service in Glasgow Cathedral at which thousands of people from the slums had been specially invited. As he spoke, he wrote later, there were moments when he found it hard to believe that the experience was real. Here he was, Hugh Redwood, preaching in a famous cathedral to an enormous congregation. Just a few years before he had not even been a Christian disciple! He knew that it was one of those tremendous privileges — honours, even — he should have thrown away had he been allowed to follow his own ideas of Christian service.

When, in 1936, he undertook a month's evangelistic tour in Canada and the United States (having received leave, on full pay, from Fleet Street) he fulfilled more than sixty speaking engagements and preached to large congregations, one, in the

Maple Leaf Gardens in Toronto, of no fewer than 12,000 people.

* * *

But the really important thing, so far as Hugh was concerned, was not that *God in the Slums* opened up wider fields of service for him, which was important and which he valued, but that other people were affected by its message. It heartened, inspired, challenged and changed the lives of many around the world, who saw through its pages that God is indeed a God of miracles, and that miracles could happen not only to the slum dwellers, but to all who believe — to *themselves*! This never ceased to amaze and humble Hugh. A missionary on furlough from the East showed him a copy of the book and it bore on its fly-leaf twelve autographs. Each name, he was told, was that of a person convinced and converted through reading it, out there in China.

Another missionary was fighting the 'twin devils'. of loneliness and doubt on the prairies of the Far West, and was saved from forsaking his post and his people by reading the records of the miracles of the slums.

A man 'high in the councils of State on the other side of the world', Hugh learned, had been so impressed with the story, and in particular with the slum children who figure in it so frequently, that he decided to relinquish his influential post and devote himself to work among needy children.

Alejandro Guzman, a Methodist convert who knew nothing of The Salvation Army, had organised religious work in Mexico City which had some Army features about it. Somehow a copy of Hugh's book fell into Guzman's hands, brought him into contact with the Army and eventually he and his work were received as part of the International Movement. In October 1937, General Evangeline Booth, conducting a campaign in Atlanta, presented an Army flag to the now *Captain* Guzman for use in Mexico City (*No Discharge in This War*, Frederick Coutts).

*   *   *

Betty Thorne was one whose life was changed through reading Hugh's book. An Anglican, she had heard of the work of The Salvation Army, and approved. But so far as she was concerned, her own loved communion had her undivided loyalty. 'The church's ancient buildings, hallowed liturgy and settled place in the nation's life seemed to make it natural that Betty, of typical English stock and culture, should be one of her loyal daughters' (*Sure of Her Call*, Emma Davies).

As Betty read *God in the Slums*, however, she realised that God was calling her into the Army. Her friends could not understand, some were not pleased, but she obeyed her call and that obedience was to take her into varied, demanding, exciting fields of service.

Too old to enter training to become an officer, she served as a helper, eventually being given the rank of Sergeant in the Goodwill Department. A skilled driver and mechanic (in the First World War she had driven Jellicoe, Beatty and Wemyss to and from duty and knew her way in and out of Buckingham Palace), she often drove Hugh to his Salvation Army appointments. In *God in the Everyday* he described how she one day surprised her fellow workers by curing the apparently incurable engine of an ancient delivery van and driving it triumphantly round a field. In the Goodwill car, an old Ford V8, on the windscreen of which were affixed the words: 'Our God is with us everywhere we go!', she covered the country from

John o'Groats to Land's End in the interests of Salvation Army work.

Given the rank of Captain in 1938, she became the companion and secretary to Major (later Commissioner) Emma Davies and with her shared appointments at Middlesbrough and Northampton. A post at the International Headquarters preceded her appointment to Ceylon (now Sri Lanka) as Candidates Secretary and Young Women's Counsellor in 1947. However, two years later, it was found that she was seriously ill and her only hope of life was to return to England. But recovery was not realised, and shortly afterwards she answered the last great call – but without fear.

Then there was the amazing result in the life of Doreen Gemmel, another miracle wrought through Hugh's record of miracles. Doreen was a sophisticated young woman, daughter of a well-to-do doctor father and a pleasure-loving socialite mother. She lived life to the full, the kind of life that was possible only to one in her privileged position. One day she came upon a copy of *God in the Slums* and received a devastating revelation of the emptiness of her life. She had heard someone mention the book in her presence some time before and later noticed a copy on a bookstall near a Glasgow railway station. Having nothing to occupy her that afternoon she paid her shilling (5p) and took the book with her to the restaurant where she had planned to have tea. She read about the young women, many of them about her own age, who of their own choice were living in the squalor of the slums 'cheerfully caring for old sick people, cleaning filthy rooms, stretching out a helping hand whenever it was needed'. She read how those women had challenged the man who had written the book and she was challenged herself. What was she doing with *her* life?

She was led to offer for service with The Salvation Army and spent nine exciting weeks living and working with Slum officers in Edinburgh. Later, as a Church Army sister, she established a refuge and shelter near Marble Arch, in London, for degraded, restless women, which was known as Bethany. Her story, to which Hugh contributed the foreword, has been told by Phyllis Thompson in *Within a Yard of Hell*; as moving a story of a modern miracle as one could read anywhere – and it happened because of *God in the Slums*.

Hugh took a real interest in Bethany, and for nearly thirty years, until a week or so before his death, kept up a lively correspondence with Sister Gemmel – his 'little sister', he called her — often sending cheques, as he felt God guided him to help with her work. He always felt profoundly grateful that he had had something to do with the establishing of so fine a work as Bethany.

*   *   *

An important result of *God in the Slums* was the formation of the Goodwill League. Again, Hugh said, this was the brain-child of Lieutenant-Colonel Colbourne. It was an attempt to co-ordinate the offers of service which the book evoked. Membership of the League would be open to all, people of any denominational affiliation and those of none. Each would give what he or she could in time, talent or substance to alleviate the plight of the needy, and it would all be organised by the officers of the slums in the district in which the member lived.

The League was inaugurated by General Edward Higgins in a great meeting at the Royal Albert Hall, in London, in October 1930, just a few weeks after the appearance of the book which started it all, and Hugh was appointed the first President.

Described by him as 'a crusade of determined friendliness', the League was not intended to be a new department within The Salvation Army but 'something embracing its entire organisation, making for better and more intimate relations with other parts of God's Church, infecting them with the "Blood and Fire" spirit, and creating a salvation spearhead for the great Christian Army of liberation!'

That was the dream! It was realised in some places when professional people — doctors, nurses, schoolteachers, solicitors, university students — as well as unemployed men, old-age pensioners and others who were themselves poor in worldly goods, gave all kinds of valuable assistance to the slum workers, employing their skills and time to help those who could profit from them. Many more gave money, and the work, founded and sustained on faith, prayer and love, grew considerably.

However, the plan was not fully worked out, not as Hugh and those associated with him envisaged in the first place. He said that the 'moulding of circumstances' gave it a form different from that of the dream. 'It came down from the heights of vision,' wrote Hugh, 'and was more and more regarded as merely an auxiliary of the Slum Department. As such, despite its limited numbers, it accomplished much valuable work and learned equally valuable lessons.'

The full story of the Goodwill League cannot be told here. That would require a book of itself, and a totally absorbing and challenging book it would be. Suffice it to say that today Goodwill units — not to be confused with the Goodwill centres, the Slum Posts of yesterday — operate within the orbit of some

Salvation Army corps in Great Britain. These are linked with the Goodwill Department and operate under the general supervision of an Organising Secretary at National Headquarters.

Their function is similar to, though not on the scale of the original dream. Salvationists and others join together under the direction of the corps Commanding Officer to visit institutions of various kinds, the sick, the bereaved and the lonely. They are ready to serve in any local emergency, to organise handicraft classes and club nights where there are those who would benefit from them. A Goodwill Sunday is held once a year when aged and handicapped people are specially invited and brought along to the meetings. In all corps, including those where a Goodwill unit does not operate, special collections are taken up on Goodwill Sunday to help goodwill work generally. The motto for the Goodwill League at corps level is that chosen in 1930: 'Such as I have give I' (Acts 3: 6).

In his capacity as President, Hugh travelled extensively in Britain visiting many Goodwill Centres, involving himself in the work and encouraging others to do the same. At the wheel of the Goodwill car Hugh was able to use for many of these engagements, was Senior-Major Stanley Burton, a valued companion and friend. For his assistance in many ways over many years, Hugh was always grateful. 'What would I do without Stanley Burton,' he used to say.

In the News Letter for November, 1943, Hugh wrote of visiting Falmouth Road, Bethnal Green, Paddington, Hoxton in London (of which more presently) and West Bromwich, Coventry and Exeter further afield. He was struck, he said, with the reflection that Exeter, Coventry and West Bromwich were all war-time openings. 'Goodwill has known no black-out, and the blitz has given us a larger place on the map than we ever had before.'

*   *   *

One centre Hugh used to visit frequently was at Bath, and it was situated in the heart of that city's worst slum, in Corn Street. Senior-Major Ella Cates, now retired and still living in the city in which she worked for so many years as a Slum officer, clearly remembers Hugh's first visit. She was a young Captain, not long out of the officers' training college, and her senior officer sent her to meet Hugh's train and escort him to the Slum Post which he was to visit to collect material for his book. 'He will be wearing a large silver shield on his coat,' she was told.

It was raining hard when the train came in but Major Cates spotted Hugh immediately, a portly Pickwickian figure in a navy blue mackintosh that reached almost to his ankles. The silver shield was there, shining its message that the wearer belonged to The Salvation Army — though, strictly speaking, in Hugh's case not as a full member, but as a greatly valued associate.

That first visit to Bath, in 1929, when Hugh did gather valuable material for his book, was followed by many more. The elegant city of Beau Nash and the famous crescents attracted him, though more on account of the Christ-motivated work he saw in the slums than for anything else. He became well known in the city and was often asked to preach in some of its churches, and he frequently led meetings at the Salvation Army corps there. Crowds attended to listen to this man with a message. But it was at the Slum Post that he enjoyed himself the most.

He used to chuckle over one incident that occurred during one visit to Corn Street. There was a knock at the door and Hugh went to answer it. He found an old lady there, a gaily coloured hat being the most impressive feature of her apparel. She had a bottle in her hand. 'Can you let me have a drop o' the red, please?' she asked. Hugh had no idea what 'a drop o' the red' might be, and it had to be explained by the officers, to whom he turned for advice, that this was the popular name applied to a certain preparation dispensed by Dr. Philip Knowles, who freely gave his services at the Slum Post as a member of the Goodwill League. It is highly likely that the benefits of 'the red' were chiefly psychological, but the slum dwellers were convinced that it did them good, as indeed it did. From then on 'a drop o' the red' was a joke with Hugh Redwood whenever he visited Bath.

He never forgot his first meeting with a very dirty old man who used to attend the Slum Post meetings there. The officers were always glad to see him, of course, but there was one problem: no other member of the congregation would sit anywhere near him, for rather obvious reasons. It was embarrassing all round. But Hugh took him in hand, led him gently to a bath-room and while the meeting proceeded administered the treatment he had required for so long. After that the old man said he would like a bath every week, please! Hugh, an occasional visitor, said he would not be able to oblige so often but when he was in the city he would be glad to do so.

Miss M. B. Hill, a wealthy lady who, when she died left her large beautiful home for use by the Army's Goodwill Department, was a tireless member of the Bath Goodwill League. She and Hugh became great friends. 'If you are Big Brother,' she said one day, 'I will be Big Sister,' and from that time she was known by that name. When she saw Hugh's large silver shield she said she would like one too, and, like Hugh, she wore it thereafter with pride.

A Slum Post clinic, originally the brain-child of Miss Hill and Dr. Knowles — she financing it and he conducting it for many years — is still continued, and is held at Whiteways Goodwill Centre, which replaced the old Corn Street Slum Post, every Tuesday and Thursday.

*   *   *

When, on the site of an old chapel occupied by the Army, and from which slum work had been operated for some years, a purpose-built Goodwill Centre was opened at Hoxton in 1939, Hugh was present as President of the Goodwill League, and took part in the inaugural proceedings by reading a Scripture portion — appropriately from Psalm 127: 'Except the Lord build the house, they labour in vain that build it . . .'

He took a close interest in the activities at Hoxton which catered for almost every need, from meals for the hungry to workrooms for men and women, a get-fit-keep-fit-club, the services of chiropodists, doctors, legal advisers, an animal clinic and emergency flats for stranded families.

Hugh saw Hoxton as a pattern for centres in every large town in the country. Run by local churches as joint enterprises, he said, they might help to change the dream of church unity into a living and working reality. It was part of the dream that did not materialise: for one thing within a few months of the opening of Hoxton, Europe was plunged into a war that was to last for six long years, so expansion such as Hugh envisaged was out of the question.

Nevertheless, the fine tradition still continues to this day at

Hoxton itself. With the support of the local government authorities, a group of dedicated officers and employees work to provide a whole range of greatly needed amenities. No fewer than 12,000 people use the centre annually and there is a mothers' and babies' club, an advice bureau, a library, a day-centre, a youth-centre, an old folks' club, as well as a twice weekly soup run in the early hours of the morning to people who live rough and sleep out. And, as for many years, a chiropodist still calls! Hugh would be happy with what Hoxton is doing today, and proud to have had some part in it during his own life-time.

*   *   *

Another important venture with which Hugh was closely associated, and which came into operation following the publication of *God in the Slums*, was the House o' the Trees. A large house and forty odd acres of land were acquired and established as an industrial and agricultural training centre for youth at Penygraig in the Welsh Valleys. This was an instant success. Those were the days of the great depression in the coal industry and the House o' the Trees experiment provided a life-line for many young men, not only by occupying them usefully since there were no jobs in the pits for them to go to, and mining was all they knew, but by helping them to acquire new skills with which they would have a better chance of finding employment elsewhere. The name 'House o' the Trees' was taken, by the way, because each boy who worked there in those first days took as a personal emblem a tree — erect and reaching upward.

House o' the Trees No. 1 was opened in March 1932. No. 2 came a year later at Pontypridd in the Taff Valley, but this was

closed after about five years, though in its time it did a fine job
with similar work: the great drawback with this was that it was
only a house, there was no surrounding land, and the range of
its accomplishments was limited.

A year after the first House o' the Trees was opened a report
was issued which said:

> Fine crops have been raised this year by miners' sons who
> thought themselves born only for the pit. Three prizes for
> produce, and a special diploma for carrots, have been won at
> a local show; and pedigree pigs and prize poultry have pro-
> vided additional work and interest. Those with other tastes
> have found an outlet, and a Cardiff firm is buying all the
> wood work their young hands are devising. Gambling loafers
> have become eager workers, healthy interests have replaced
> blank hours. One youth walks early across the mountains and
> tends the hens before four in the morning.
>
> Regular hours, good meals and an object in life have
> brought about a great improvement in physique, but the
> most gladdening change in these youths lies in their new
> loyalties. In the first hour of their arrival each was invited to
> join hands with us in faith and prayer: for we have no work
> to report which is merely a social effort.

Lieutenant-Colonel David Wolfe, now retired, was an em-
ployee at the House o' the Trees before he became a Salvation
Army officer, and was present at the opening ceremony. He
recalls that Hugh spoke, and made a considerable impression
on that occasion. The Colonel remembers Hugh's many subsequent visits. The House o' the Trees, he says, was quite
special to Hugh, a work after his own heart, one in which he
took a keen active interest.

Later, with changing circumstances, the House o' the Trees was adapted to cope with the problems of juvenile delinquency. Courts in many parts of Britain began to send their toughest problems to Penygraig and, to prove that in many of these boys the grace of God wrought miracles, Hugh put on record that he later actually shared the same pulpit with one or two of them, and there was one lad who gave a ringing testimony to a congregation which included his one-time captor, the police superintendent. 'The House o' the Trees', he wrote, 'deals with its problem cases by converting them.'

With Home Office support and operating under the direction of the Men's Social Services of The Salvation Army, the House o' the Trees continues its work with young offenders against the law, staffed by a team of Salvation Army officers and trained social workers. There is accommodation for sixteen boys.

* * *

Yet another aspect of Goodwill work in which Hugh was greatly interested was the work of the officers among the hop-fields of Kent and Worcestershire. Every year, at the appropriate season, people from the slums would accept the offer of work in the hop-fields, and whole families would go together and live there for a few weeks in huts provided by the farmers. They had to work hard at a tiring job and were not overpaid, but, in fact, this was the only 'holiday' many of them had. It was their great annual exodus from the slums to adventure in the country. Where the people went, there would the Slum officers go.

Work among the hop-pickers began as early as 1886 when a brigade of twelve officers from the slums accompanied a group of pickers to the Kent fields. The work developed until, when

Hugh came into the picture, slum dwellers were going to the hop-fields in their thousands. Some years the slums were almost deserted. Hugh was a frequent and popular visitor to the hop-fields, and he was frankly critical of the conditions under which some of the workers had to live. He wrote:

> With a few notable exceptions . . . the pickers are housed like animals. As a rule they bring with them their entire households and all their household goods; and these are crowded into a hut which is, ordinarily, a single compartment of wood or stone, without windows, fitments or furnishings. Six or more people of both sexes may live in a hut, sleeping together on the straw which the farmer is required to provide, or on a mattress they have brought with them.

But the Army was there, to bring love and care, and the gospel.

On a Saturday night in 1932, at one Kentish hop-field, fifty-seven babies were bathed by three officers, while nine open-air meetings at different points were holding the attention of men and women who had been arrested on their way to the public-houses by the gospel message in testimony or song. The bathing of these babies was not so simple as it sounds, for the water had to be carried across a field and up a lane, a task unlikely to be undertaken by the respective mothers, especially after twelve hours in the fields.

Hugh wrote:

> Hopping without the Army . . . would be almost unthinkable. The roughest and vilest respect it, the traffic obeys its signals, the publican sighs with relief when its stentorian opposition outside silences the disorder in his bar room. Its

presence stems the licence of the weekends when every other restraint is in danger of being swept away. The circle of its open-air worship is never broken and on Saturday nights and Sundays, when it is reinforced by London bandsmen with their glittering instruments of war, the drunks and semi-drunks will press around it, joining in the singing, baring their heads during prayer, and now and then, in individual cases, kneeling in sudden soberness to pray for themselves at the drum-head (*God in the Slums*).

And how Hugh loved to be involved in all this. It was, he said, the Salvation Army of the Hallelujah days; fearless, rejoicing, uncompromising; the Army of Whitechapel and the Mile End Waste, 'at grips with elemental passion in the dust and the mud of the highway'.

Hugh was always moved when he heard the 'hop-pickers' anthem', as it was called. Picture the Army Captain holding an evening open-air meeting. She stands, or kneels, with a concertina in her hands, leading the singing, and the mums, dads, and children of the slums joined in reverently, moved and mellowed by the atmosphere of what is truly a holy place where God is.

The 'anthem', as Hugh, with his love of words and music, could not help observing, had little literary or musical merit, but it gained, he said, a certain beauty both from the surroundings and the singing:

> God is with us all the time,
> In the morning when joybells chime;
> In the evening when lights are low;
> Our God is with us everywhere we go.

With all this activity Hugh tirelessly associated himself. There was much more. There were the holiday homes the Army established at such places as Herne Bay where, at Resthaven, tired women from the slums could go for a few sweet, heavenly days. There was Sunshine Lodge at Yalding in the Weald of Kent, this time for children. There was Tankerton, by the sea, a rest and holiday haven for mothers and children. In all this fine work Hugh took a lively and active interest. Then there were numerous day excursions organised by the Slum officers to bring a little brightness into drab, empty lives — a day at the seaside from the slums of London was then a day to remember. Hugh shared enthusiastically in it all.

CHAPTER 8

Man of Letters, and Much More

IT IS TRUE that in writing, as in all creative pursuits, any gift a man may possess must be developed by hard work. There is no easy way to success even for those who have been generously endowed by nature. This was true for Hugh Redwood. That he had a gift for writing is plain. He possessed outstanding powers of description, could handle words with rare skill, was master of the apt, well-rounded, unforgettable phrase. But he had to serve a long, hard apprenticeship in order to perfect his craft.

His first training, as a cub-reporter on the *Western Daily Press* was in gathering news and the factual reporting of it. There was no encouragement from his mentors of those early days to write descriptive pieces: it was the news itself that mattered, and so long as it was accurately, lucidly and economically recorded it was satisfactory. There was no call for verbal ornamentation.

But Hugh had not been launched very long upon his career before this approach began to irk. He wanted to give his rising powers fuller rein. He baulked at having to begin even routine reporting — of an inquest, say — in the same unimaginative, stereotyped style, and then continue to the end of the piece in the way that such pieces had, for generations past, been continued to the end. He wanted to report the facts, report them accurately, but to vary the means, to devise different openings, and to produce, he hoped, added interest for the reader.

One day he did venture a deviation from the accustomed style, an attempt to bring what he considered greatly needed freshness into the sober news columns. It was far from being a major revolution, but his editor did not appreciate it. He was called into the great man's office and told, with appropriate finger-pointing gestures, to kindly remember he was a reporter, and not a leader-writer!

For some time thereafter, since his job depended on it, Hugh kept to the well-trodden paths and before long was well on the way to 'dullness and disillusion' as he put it. It was sad for him at the time, but not without its long-term compensations. The discipline did him good. Later on he developed a style of his own, breaking some of the rules that had been hammered home in those early days, but by then, of course, he knew them thoroughly.

Each stage of his early career made its own contribution to the development of his chosen profession. His graduation to *pro tem* music critic of his paper was a step in the right direction. Here some style was called for, and Hugh was able to let himself go a little.

Then later there came a period with the Central News Agency when he had to learn the art of expanding incoming telegrams, and also, in order to save as much money as possible, to condense the messages going out, without, in the first case, reading too much into the outline and, in the second, without omitting vital matter. All this added to his writing experience as nothing else could have done, and helped shape the future author of successful books.

He wrote more than a score, some of them now largely forgotten. They served a useful purpose at the time they appeared, but are unlikely to be revived. Hugh would not have been surprised at that, nor disappointed. But others still hold interest for today's reader. One of these is his first and most successful book, *God in the Slums*. As we saw in the last chapter he wrote this with his heart and it reached the hearts of hundreds of thousands around the world. It is still worth reading after forty-five years.

In his second book Hugh essayed something different, though the style is undeniably Redwood. Writing in the third person, with the hero's name given as Peter Rawlins, Hugh delivered a thinly-disguised account of his own spiritual pilgrimage up to that time, 1932. He called the book *God in the Shadows*, for he dealt at length with the dark experience of personal sorrow in the illness of his daughter Gwen (called Daphne in this book), how he came out of it, and with what result to himself. It was issued in a format similar to that of his first book, with another striking Hogarthian jacket designed by Frank Brangwyn. This book also had a wide sale, and ran to many reprints.

A steady stream of books now flowed from his lively pen. There was *Kingdom Come*, a study in the Lord's Prayer. This was not a theological exposition, for Hugh was not, and would never have claimed to be a theologian. The book was, as he said, 'an attempt to set down in correlation' the major lessons of the years since his conversion, the years of his involvement with The Salvation Army — then about eight. He said that in the

Lord's Prayer, as he looked at it through the eyes of a journalist, he found illustrations of what following Christ should mean to the individual. The book, which is replete with stories from his practical Goodwill work in the slums, is at once challenging and heartening. This is probably one of those that are not read much now, having gone out of print years ago; this is a pity, since it still has valid things to say to the present generation about Christian discipleship, and the way to exercise it in the world. Of course, many of the illustrations are of necessity dated, though there is no doubt that these stories still make interesting and heart-moving reading.

God in the Everyday and *Practical Prayer* came next, in 1936 and 1937 respectively. The former was the outcome of a suggestion that he should write a book to tell men and women how to find God, under the title, *The Pathway to God*. The request was of itself revealing of the wide influence of a man who, less than ten years before, had been unconverted and, outside his immediate circle, quite unknown. He accepted the idea for the book, but not the title: this he considered too dogmatic. He believed that while 'for the Christian there is but one way to God, the approaches to Jesus are numberless and must vary as every man's individual position varies'. So, as in *Kingdom Come* Hugh took his readers through the Lord's Prayer, in *God in the Everyday* he took them through life: God in Youth, in Experience, in Business, in Adversity, in Prayer — are some of the chapter titles. It is a serious book, as one reviewer said, a book that confronts Christian and sceptic alike with straight questions that demand straight answers. Like all Hugh's books, it is written in simple, everyday language and there surely, along with his skilfully handled, straight-from-life illustrations, lies the secret of its persuasiveness.

Practical Prayer was written ten years and some months after the 'supreme crisis' of Hugh's life. In ten years he had learned a great deal about prayer: he had studied it, he had experimented with it, but he nevertheless considered himself to be a beginner, and the book he set out to write was to be a book for beginners. It is indeed that, but it is also a book from which the mature Christian can profit. In the matter of prayer are not all of us, the most experienced of us, still learning? Hugh wrote about the theory and the practice of prayer; about private and public prayer. And what sanctified common sense he employed! He believed in keeping records of his prayer requests and card indexes of his prayer subjects. He felt that prayer was too serious a matter to be treated in a haphazard fashion. *Practical Prayer* leaves no one in any doubt about that. It is in many ways a simple book, there are in fact many profound and sound ideas and suggestions in it, some of which could well be explored profitably today, nearly forty years later.

In 1946 Hugh issued a book that was quite different from anything he had previously written. It was a study of the Fourth Gospel with the title *The Book of Lazarus*. His Bible studies had persuaded him that the man Jesus raised from the dead, the brother of Mary and Martha of Bethany, was the author of the Fourth Gospel and that it was authenticated by John the Apostle, or possibly by John and Peter. He sets out clearly the evidence for this conclusion and while, as he expected, not everybody will agree with his conclusions, the examining of the evidence for them is a rewarding exercise.

The second half of this book consists of a very free paraphrase of the whole of the Gospel under review, though he was not a New Testament scholar and had no intention of trying to produce a scholarly work. He wanted his effort to be regarded as the attempt of a newspaper man to present the best of all news in the style of a daily newspaper. Readers will have to judge whether he succeeded: they may feel J. B. Phillips and *The Living Bible* have more recently done a better job. Nevertheless, comparing Hugh's rendering with the Authorised Version and other modern translations, one finds some illuminating phrases.

Many would agree that his most accomplished book, his most literary work, was his straight autobiography, *Bristol Fashion.* Published in 1948, it had behind it the experience of many years of writing and of Christian discipleship. It is mature in its reflections on the events of life in general as well as his own personal life. It is a remarkably detailed account of the times in which he lived, those tumultuous and momentous times from his earliest years before the turn of the twentieth century to the end of the Second World War. As a journalist he was closely involved in the happenings at home and abroad of those decades and had personal connections with a surprising number of the chief participants. His comments on some of these leading personalities are penetrating and make fascinating reading. *Bristol Fashion* is a book to interest the historian. But he wrote chiefly to chronicle his own spiritual pilgrimage and in the doing of it gave glory to the God of all grace who put His hand upon him and who, through rebellion and near-denial, through doubt and failing, never left him and brought him at last into a deep relationship with Himself, giving him a large place of service in His eternal Kingdom. This book had a deservedly wide sale.

His last book in fact, though he did make plans for another, was *Residue of Days*, written after a miraculous recovery from a serious illness which doctors had pronounced terminal. He was brought back to life again, however, and wrote the book in his seventy-fifth year — hence the title. It is a book of hope; one man's testimony to the boundless power and grace of God. It is a confession of faith, by one who had passed through bright days and dark, that God is dependable and that prayer works. It is a glowing testimony to divine guidance and to a love that never fails.

The book he planned and did not live to write was completed by his friend and colleague, Alfred Angel, under the title *Stop Press*. A good deal of Hugh himself went into this slim volume: chapters he had already written; a series of prayer thoughts; a collection of his One-Minute Sermons.

These One-Minute Sermons, which became so far-reaching an aspect of his writing ministry, call for some explanation. They were born out of adversity, economic adversity in Fleet Street. For some time, as Religious Editor, Hugh had contributed a short sermon to the Saturday page of the *News Chronicle*, running to around two hundred words. But when Fleet Street was hit by an economic blizzard — one of the many with which it has been afflicted in modern times — it was decreed that the religious features would have to go and with them, possibly, his job. Those in power had decided that religion was not good news value, but they were to be proved wrong. Hugh was against cutting religion out of the paper, pleaded with his editor for a reprieve, and a compromise was reached. He was told that if he reduced his weekly sermons by one half, to one hundred words including the text, one could appear every Saturday on the paper's feature page. Those One Minute Sermons, as they were called, were an immediate success, a much greater success than the longer items which preceded them and out of which they came. And Hugh retained his position on the editorial staff. When, after Hugh's retirement, the *News Chronicle* closed and was taken over by the *Daily Mail*, the feature was retained by the new editor and it continued to appear until a few days before Hugh's death.

Yet another highly successful feature that Hugh contributed to his newspaper was 'Today's Parable'. It was just after *God in the Slums* had burst upon a surprised and appreciative public that Hugh was called into Tom Clarke's office and asked if he could not get the *God in the Slums* touch into the paper. The idea Clarke had in mind was that a simple sentence, embracing a helpful thought, should appear every day at the foot of the leader column. He wanted something to which readers would turn every day when they took up their newspaper; something to give them a tonic, or make them laugh or occasionally make them angry. Hugh was the man to do it, Clarke decided, and he was right. Hugh began, and thereafter provided a daily parable for eight years, and the feature became extremely popular, greatly valued by countless numbers of people who would have by-passed a larger piece. The ten, fifteen, twenty words suited them fine.

Many of these items were not obviously 'religious'. Said one such:

Pet subjects, if taken out in public, should always be kept on a lead.

And another:

Rough edges spoil the smoothest lawns, and the smoothest tongues as well.

Others were more direct in their application of spiritual truth:

God is so often an unannounced caller that He knows all the excuses for keeping Him on the doorstep.

God points a man like a pencil, cutting away his outer self and baring that with which He may make His mark.

Several collections of these were later published in book form.

So Hugh's pen was kept busy. With it he earned his bread and butter; with it he exercised a wide-reaching, Kingdom-building ministry. He was in great demand to write articles for religious journals, and a number of The Salvation Army's publications were enriched by his lively contributions.

*   *   *

Not only his pen, but also his voice was used extensively in the service of his Lord. We have seen how he was launched upon his preaching ministry following *God in the Slums,* and how wide a ministry developed from that first invitation to occupy a church pulpit, or, to go back further still, from those first attempts at giving homely talks in Slum Post meetings. Were these not his first excursions into public speaking for Christ? Or should we go back even further, to those Bristol days when the newly-converted eighteen-year-old was invited to 'give his testimony', and was also occasionally asked to accompany and assist more experienced Salvationists when they visited nearby centres to lead Sunday meetings?

The day came, however, when Hugh was invited to broadcast. Frank Cobb, a journalist working in the publicity department of the BBC, remembers going into the office of the then head of the Corporation's religious department, the Rev. (now the Venerable Archdeacon of Macclesfield) Francis House, and saying: 'Why don't we do something about Hugh Redwood? He would be just right for "Lift ups" '! (*Lift up your Hearts* was a regular and highly popular early-morning five-minute series of talks given by various speakers.) In due course Hugh was approached, and before long he was a regular and successful contributor to the programme.

Where did the secret lie? Certainly not in his voice. He possessed, as someone said who knew him well, and respected him greatly, 'a throaty, drawling voice'. There was something else; something far more important and that something cancelled out any disadvantage his rather unattractive voice might have carried. The Rev. Elsie Chamberlain, who was Assistant Head of Religious Broadcasting at the time, and who knew Hugh well, puts her finger on it. She writes: 'When he wrote his scripts for broadcasting it was always for the help and comfort of particular people he had in mind and in prayer. Their names or initials were in the corners of the scripts he used for the broadcasts. I think this is why there were always so many others who thought that what he had said was just for them. He was so gently but directly personal.'

*　　*　　*

Apart from Hugh's association with The Salvation Army, with which Movement he without doubt exercised the major portion of his Christian discipleship, he had a close and active connection with other religious bodies. He was, and remained until the end of his days, a member of the Anglican communion, and as such was a licensed lay-reader in the diocese of Rochester. The Lord Bishop of Tonbridge, The Right Rev. Russell B. White, was one of the speakers, representing a number of denominations, who paid tribute to Hugh in a memorial service in London a few weeks after his death.

But despite his strong Anglican affiliation his closest active association, he said, was with the Free Churches. He was often present at their conferences and loved to get accounts of such into his newspaper. He was elected to the Executive of the National Free Church Council (later the Free Church Federal Council) though not on account of any particular affiliation with them, as he pointed out, but simply because of the unique nature of his work — as religious editor of a national newspaper as well as his 'voluntary' work for the whole Church of Christ. It was no doubt an unusual thing for an Anglican to be invited to serve such a body. He was also for a time the National President of the Brotherhood Movement, an interdenominational association of brotherhoods, sisterhoods and kindred societies seeking to unite its members into a nation-wide fraternity of Christian fellowship and practical service.

The Movement began in 1875 when a John Blackman, an earnest Christian worker, deacon of Ebenezer Congregational Church, West Bromwich, was moved to organise meetings for working men who, he had observed, did not often associate themselves with the Church. The movement spread, first in Britain, where initially the meetings were known as Pleasant Sunday Afternoons (or P.S.A.), and then overseas.

It was in 1938 that Hugh accepted nomination by the National Conference of the association to become the National President for the following year, and he went on to serve a second term in 1940, following in office such men as Sir Isaac Foot, the Rev. Canon 'Dick' Sheppard and Lord Inman.

The present General Secretary, Mr. A. E. H. Gregory, recalls his pleasure at serving under Hugh, and says that 'he truly believed in Christian brotherhood, and his dedication to his Lord was an inspiration to all who were associated with him'.

In addition to all this he was, as we have seen, a tireless, active, innovating President of the Goodwill League.

Every moment of Hugh's days was filled up with activity. He travelled extensively, preaching the news of the Kingdom to those outside it, and bringing inspiration and illumination to those within. He wrote and he broadcast; he conducted a massive correspondence with many people in all parts of the world, people in need of counsel as well as those in need of cash: Hugh had some answer for them all. All this work he achieved in His 'spare' time, for he was still a man with heavy responsibilities in Fleet Street, and was to carry them with distinction until the day of his retirement.

It was true to say of him, and it *was* said, many times, that he was a 'good' man. The Bishop of Tonbridge said in his memorial service tribute that in a man's life 'that which matters most ... (is) what he *is*; "being" rather than "doing".' And that is undoubtedly so. But in Hugh, as in all good men, being and doing were perfectly joined, all of a piece. He was a man of many parts, a talented man, and all his parts and all his talents were fully dedicated to the God who had called him and marked out a path for him to follow.

CHAPTER 9

Man of Faith

IN 1933, TOM CLARKE, editor of the *News Chronicle*, and Hugh's chief, announced that he was to resign. Hugh was genuinely sorry. The two men had worked together since 1926 when Clarke, then the news editor of the *Daily Mail* and one of Lord Northcliffe's forceful young men, joined the *Daily News* as editor. Latterly, Hugh had been Clarke's deputy, and though the two men did not always see eye to eye in matters affecting the paper, there was mutual respect between them. Hugh considered Clarke an extremely able journalist and spoke highly of his loyalty to his staff. He was glad to be not only his colleague but his friend.

There was never any thought in Hugh's mind that he would succeed his chief. He had no hankering after the post anyway, nor did he consider himself qualified to fill it, though here he may have been underestimating his capacity, for he was a newspaper man of proved ability and wide experience.

He stayed for some time as deputy to the new editor, Aylmer Vallance, until, early in 1934, he made a remarkable suggestion to his superiors. He had for some time been deputy editor in name only and this was causing him considerable frustration. What should he do? he kept asking himself. He was grateful that, despite the fact that in the new set up there was much that irked, his position did give him opportunities to pursue his religious work, and these he did not want to lose. But he began to wonder if a post could possibly be created for him on the paper in which he could *extend* his work for God? Would it be possible to combine his daily work *with* religious activity? What would the powers-that-be think if he put to them an idea that was rapidly taking form in his mind, to resign his position as deputy editor and suggest a new one for himself, one that had not before been heard of in Fleet Street, but one for which he felt there was a great need and which he was confident he could fill — that of religious editor? Religion *was* still news, he believed, and if the suggestion was accepted he would be free to handle it for his paper in all its aspects. He knew he was taking a risk. His superiors might accept his resignation but not his suggestion about a new post. What then? He was fifty years old and had a sick wife and an invalid daughter. It was a risk all right, but he knew he must take it, and his relief must have been considerable when no objection was raised at the proposal, and very soon he was happily settled in his new job.

He was to fill it with distinction for many years, until his retirement, years that were among the happiest and most rewarding, spiritually speaking, of his whole life. Through the position of religious editor he made an outstanding contribution to the paper, to journalism generally and to the cause of true religion. But he had to create the post. There was no precedent for it. He had to keep himself well informed in the whole religious field and see that what was happening was reported. He contributed three regular religious features: a weekly 'sermon', (which later became the One-Minute Sermon), a topical religious article and a daily 'parable', Tom Clarke's idea, which appeared at the foot of the leader column. This, as one commentator observed, was often more pungent than the leader itself.

An enormous correspondence resulted from all this, and Hugh had to deal with it himself because for most of the time he was without secretarial help. This correspondence included numerous requests for prayer from all kinds of people and for all manner of needs and causes, and he had to develop a comprehensive card-index system to ensure that such requests were properly dealt with. Later he was able to gather around him a group of sympathetic Christian colleagues at the office who were willing to share the burden of intercession.

He was also sent a great many monetary and other gifts and they had to be dispensed to those who had made application to Hugh for practical assistance. This aspect of the work developed rapidly, and Hugh never doubted for a moment that God was in it all. Being religious editor of a national newspaper might be his daily work, it was also a far-reaching, God-honouring ministry into which he had been led and which he felt privileged to exercise. It was all surely part of the plan which, years before, Lieutenant-Colonel Colbourne had prophesied God would make for him.

*   *   *

Hugh was a firm believer in God's guidance. He wrote that 'our Lord still gives "to every man his work", and assures him of the means to perform it', that He will 'give us guidance . . . if we honestly seek it and are ready to abide by it'.

He went even further. He believed that God will pursue a

man even in the wilderness; and he had every reason for be-
lieving that. From those early days in Bristol when he turned
his back on the gospel after that 'mild flirtation' which lasted
little more than a year, God, he believed, had followed him all
the way. His was a love that would not let him go. Towards the
end of his life Hugh wrote:

> I had alienated myself from the fold. There lay in my path a
> peril of which I had no inkling, a time of domestic sorrow
> and trial in which, without God, I could have no hope. And
> He sought me out, as I believe, in foreknowledge of it, to
> stand with me throughout the ordeal and for ever after. It
> was the Shepherd, seeking and saving the lost in the wilder-
> ness, coming between me and the fear and despair which
> might have destroyed me.

Hugh also had deep faith in the power and ability of God to
answer the prayers of His people, and he wrote a great deal on
the subject. As we have seen, he devoted a whole book to it, and
the title, *Practical Prayer*, indicates his approach.

He noted in the introduction to that book that 'even among
professing Christians there are thousands who have no experience of prayer as a science, essentially practical and based upon
law'. He set out to show that prayer is all of that. The book was
a plea to Christians to pray with heart and mind, to observe the
laws which he was firmly convinced God had established. 'Real
revival cannot come until Christians really pray,' he averred,
and the words are as true now as when he wrote them, more
than forty years ago. They are always true.

He records in his books many instances of direct and exact
answers to his own prayers for the meeting of specific needs.

Let the reader beware of meeting such stories with scepticism or, if that is too strong a word, with over-much bewilderment. Is not God a God of miracles? (Hugh, by the way, defined a miracle not as a breaking of natural law but as a revelation of a little understood spiritual law). And is not God lovingly concerned with His children's needs and hopes? Hugh's remarkable stories of answered prayers came out of his own experiences, the experiences of a good and intelligent man, and such stories must not be dismissed just because such thing rarely, if ever, happen to us. We may have to look to ourselves for reasons, to our own lack of faith. God has not changed. As the writer to the Hebrews says: 'Jesus Christ (is) the same yesterday, and today, and for ever.'

In *Kingdom Come*, Hugh wrote:

I have many times received, through the post, the exact amounts required to meet particular cases of need. Once it was for £3 for a blind boy's holiday. I was asked for it in a hurry by the secretary of a charity, and because my pocket was almost empty I very nearly missed sending it. Something pointedly reminded me that my cheque book was in my portfolio, and the money was duly forwarded. The next morning my letters included one from a friend which contained £3 'for one of your hard cases'. On another occasion it was for a like sum to buy a sorely needed push chair for crippled lads at a holiday home. It was waiting for me when I returned, enclosed in a letter from Oxford.

Hugh recorded many similar cases, and was careful to point out that they were all documented, and based on his own letter-files and book entries. He had, of course, to face the great problem with which the praying man of faith must sometimes be confronted — the problem of prayers that God appears not to answer. But Hugh did not believe true prayers ever went unanswered: sometimes they were not *granted* but that, he held, was a quite different thing. There are prayers which God ought not to hear because they ought not to have been made. And there are, he said, those people who cannot take 'no' for an answer, which is a pity, since some of God's most wonderful answers are answers in the negative. He knew that in his own life. In many cases he later saw the reason for the 'no', and where he did not he was nevertheless content, for one day, he believed, round 'the bend of the road', his vision would be extended.

Hugh felt that this was particularly true in the area of physical healing, as in the case of Gwen's illness, for though she did not die, neither did she fully recover. This was an aspect of God's work which he did not profess to understand. 'I should be less than honest', he wrote, 'if I did not admit that in (many) instances, notwithstanding earnest prayer and apparently favourable conditions, hopes of healing have not been realised. I am sure there is an explanation, but I cannot put one forward which wholly satisfies me.'

This did not shake his firm belief, however, that disease is contrary to the divine will, or that the power to heal is still at the disposal of God's people. But he was compelled to the view that divine healing is governed by laws and dependent upon conditions of which, as yet, we have little appreciation. Notwithstanding the element of deep mystery on the whole subject, he wrote of his contention that 'a gospel from which the healing of Christ is excluded is incomplete'. He also believed that physical healing was not to be emphasised as a central theme since the salvation of the soul is so much more important.

There came a day, he records, when he had to face the question as to whether the Lord was wanting to use him as a healer. He felt himself to be lacking in both knowledge and faith, yet he could not evade the question. At last he made his prayer: 'If you require a human channel for the exercise of Your power, use me, Lord, just as You will.'

He secretly hoped the Lord would not call upon him, but He did. Soon after he had made his offering, and following a service at which he had preached the sermon, he came into contact with a young man whose wife was in a mental hospital. The man was a sincere believer, but the troubles that had come upon him were affecting him profoundly. He was in danger of being swept away, he said.

Hugh felt drawn to him. He felt he had to give him some assurance, to say something that would bring him hope again. So he told him to go home and pray for his wife's recovery, and as he spoke he felt he had communicated something of his own confidence. The man went home and prayed, and Hugh, his wife, and a group of friends prayed also. Within a few months the 'miracle had happened'. The word 'miracle', Hugh said, was the right word, since the woman's doctors said that her recovery could not possibly have been the result of any treatment they had prescribed. Years afterwards Hugh was still in touch with the couple.

This was his first lesson in the school of healing. Others followed, and Hugh was greatly moved by them all. He wrote:

I do not yet know how the higher law came into action, or the exact part in its operation which I was permitted to play. Certainly not at any time did I regard it as that of a healer;

and with no requests from the sufferer, and no leading of the Spirit, the thought of anointing, of laying-on of hands did not once occur to my mind. But this I can say, and perhaps it is what matters most: all I did, little though it was, was done in the name of Jesus Christ.

*   *   *

Another area of belief on which Hugh often spoke and wrote was the life everlasting. He contributed a chapter to a symposium of essays under the general title: *Is there a life after death*? (Arthur James, Evesham), in which he set out the reasons for his belief in resurrection for mankind. It was based on his confidence that God created man for Himself and will not allow sin and death ultimately to thwart His purpose. The fall of man cannot be final because God, in love, initiated a rescue operation and those who respond to that love, that patient love, will find salvation, eternal life *now*. Since a child of God has already received eternal life, the act of physical death means only a transition from one kind of life — life on earth for which a body is necessary — to life on another, higher plane.

Hugh believed that Christ would again come to the earth, according to a literal interpretation of Acts 1: 11. But he did not pretend that there was not, to him, a whole series of unanswered or imperfectly answered questions surrounding the credal statement that He will come 'to judge the quick and the dead', though he had no doubt there was to be a judgment, to be exercised in love. He believed that happenings in the world showed that Scripture prophecy was being fulfilled and that the time of Christ's second coming was not far distant.

*   *   *

Hugh's faith in God's ability to heal and in His willingness to answer prayer was to be tested in 1933 when Edith was taken ill again. A major operation was said to be necessary and Hugh had to be prepared for the possibility that she might not recover. He steeled himself for the sad event while trying to shield his wife from the full gravity of her condition.

He did two things which somehow seemed to him contradictory and about which he had some debate in his mind. He asked Colonel (later Commissioner) William Booth Davey, a Salvation Army officer with a reputation for the gift of healing, to visit his home and pray with Edith, and the Colonel did. He also acted on the doctor's advice and applied for a hospital bed in preparation for the operation. Did this second course of action betray his lack of faith in God's ability to heal and make nonsense of his request to Colonel Davey? The question troubled him for a while.

Following the Colonel's visit there was some improvement in Edith's condition; she was easier in her mind though it was by no means certain that physical healing was to come. Nevertheless she did not need to take to her bed. On the advice of a young doctor — the son, incidentally of the H. W. Smith who had been a journalist colleague of Hugh years before and who had secured him the position on the *Daily News* when he left Central News Agency — Hugh saw another doctor who had been treating cases like Edith's with his own deep X-ray method. He had had some remarkable results, and Edith, too, responded to his treatment and recovered. Was it medical science then, and not faith in God? Hugh would have said it was both. As far as he was concerned it was another miracle in his experience.

*   *   *

Of all the contacts Hugh had around this time with well-known people in national life one of particular interest and importance should be recalled.

In 1931 Ramsay MacDonald was at the head of a National Government. It was a time of grave national crisis, and the decision had to be made to come off the gold standard. Hugh tells in *Bristol Fashion* how, along with other editors, he was required to attend at Downing Street to receive a statement on the crisis, and he found himself sitting opposite the Premier, with Stanley Baldwin on his right and Philip Snowden on his left. The Prime Minister broke the news to the assembled company, imploring them to use their influence as responsible newspaper men so that the people of Britain, and the world at large, might not think there was cause for panic.

Hugh, and doubtless others with him that day, sensed the great burden which the national leader was carrying, and he wondered how the nation's troubles could be resolved. He later felt constrained to write the Premier a note suggesting that he, as head of the Government, make an appeal to the people of Britain, and call them back to God. Hugh felt, and he wanted the national leader to see, that the only real solution to the nation's deep ills was in a return to the ways of righteousness based on a revival of religious faith. The message was received cordially but not acted upon.

However, disappointed though he undoubtedly was, Hugh felt that the way had been paved for a later approach along similar lines. After consulting with his editor, he again wrote to the Prime Minister and once more suggested an appeal to the nation. The pages of the *News Chronicle* were open to him: would he speak to the nation through them? would he be willing to discuss the matter? The Prime Minister made an immediate and positive response and Hugh was invited to Downing Street. The two men talked together for nearly an hour and by the end of their conversation Ramsay MacDonald had agreed to write a Christmas message to the people (it was then late November) if his ministerial colleagues left him sufficient peace in which to do so. Hugh provided him with a rough draft to work on, but the message was never prepared. The Premier got caught up with pressing affairs of State and Hugh received a telegram in which regret was expressed that the newspaper article could not be delivered.

Hugh was disappointed for the second time. He felt that the time was right to call the nation back to God and that Ramsay MacDonald was the man who could have done it. Hugh believed that if he had made his appeal he would have 'moved' the British people 'profoundly!' If that call had been issued Hugh would have to be credited with having played an important part in the destiny of the nation at a time of deep crisis, for the idea was his alone. It is interesting to speculate how differently the history of the nation might have developed, to affect, perhaps, the days in which we now live, if Hugh's suggestion had been acted upon.

* * *

During these years of the thirties Hugh continued to travel in his Master's service. There were countless preaching engagements up and down the British Isles, in Salvation Army centres and churches of every denomination. Hugh was a well-known and greatly-respected figure in the religious life of Britain, and his 1936 tour of Canada and the U.S.A. — which we noted in an earlier chapter — indicated that his influence had spread even further afield.

CHAPTER 10

The Closing Years

FOLLOWING EDITH'S RECOVERY, Hugh took her to Scotland for a second honeymoon, and they had a marvellous time revisiting the places which had brought them such happiness years before. It was all something to wonder at: a short time ago Edith had been given a few months to live, but here she was enjoying life to the full. In fact she was to be at Hugh's side for a further five years, years which, for Hugh, were crowded with work, journalistic and evangelistic. Edith could not literally join him in all he was doing for, notwithstanding her new lease of life, she had to be careful not to overtax herself. But she followed his every movement and rejoiced at his every success. The days when she had appeared not to be able to understand all his out-of-the-office activities seemed now to be in the past, and the last five years they spent together were possibly among the happiest of their married life.

They were not without their anxieties, however. Hugh thought that before 1937 had ended Edith suspected the truth about her physical condition and that her recovery was not to be too long-lasting. The doctors had won a battle, as Hugh put it, but not the war. For them and for her it was not all over.

During the next few months she displayed remarkable for-
titude and Hugh wrote about her with deep affection and
marked admiration. He could think of no finer example of
human courage, he said, than that which Edith showed during
1938, the last year of her life. 'If she was short of breath, it was
only a "touch" of asthma; if a stab of pain betrayed itself in her
face, it was only a "touch" of cramp.'

There was obviously not much time left; she was not to see
the start of what was to be the greatest war in the history of
mankind. Towards the end of that year, during which Neville
Chamberlain came back from Munich with his promise of
'peace in our time', Edith was admitted to hospital. By Christmas she was seriously ill, though she made a gallant endeavour
not to spoil the festive season for Hugh and Gwen. The effort
was too much for her, however, and hastened the end, Hugh
thought. On New Year's Day she died.

Not far away during these anxious times was the ever-faith-
ful Elsie, a very present help in trouble. She had been around,
of course, for years. Hugh had come to rely on her for much. He
felt he should always need her by him, and Gwen thought so
too. She had her own dear companion, Ivy; her father, she was
convinced, needed Elsie more than ever now that Edith had
gone, and she besought him not to face the future alone. In
August, therefore, just as the war was to take the world into
tragedy and loss, Hugh made a great gain. He and Elsie were
married.

*   *   *

If, as Hugh said, the First World War passed him by, the
second certainly did not. But then, no one in Britain escaped

the effects of it. As never before in history, the death and devastation of nations in conflict were brought to the very front doors of the people.

Hugh, in common with thousands of his fellow workers, took his regular turn at fire-watching in the city, though he was never on duty during a major raid. But the *News Chronicle* building, where he worked, did not escape the enemy's bombs. Part of the office was struck by a high explosive in May 1941 and though it could have been much worse — and would have been on any other night but a Saturday, when the building was almost empty — a great deal of machinery was lost and the paper had for a time to be printed elsewhere.

One night in 1944 the war came even closer. The house in Orpington, where the family was living by then, having moved from Catford just before the outbreak of hostilities, was badly affected by a flying-bomb which landed only a hundred yards away. It was shortly after five in the morning. Hugh had just left the shelter where he and Elsie had spent the night, and entered the house to make some tea when the bomb fell. He thought the end had come, and in that terrible moment the words of the 'hop-pickers' anthem' came back to him, 'God is with us all the time . . .' and he knew he was in the best hands of all. His next thought was that perhaps he had been blinded, for the blood was streaming over his eyes and everything was black. But he was in fact only cut about the face with flying glass, and was suffering from severe shock. Elsie was safe in the shelter, and Gwen was safer still in Somerset where, with Ivy, she had been evacuated for the duration of the war.

The damage to the house was extensive but not beyond repair. The services — gas, electricity, telephone — still functioned, and the furniture was not destroyed. Characteristically Hugh found a Bible text which, to him, was appropriate to the occasion. He looked about him at the sorry mess, and, a touch of jocosity mingling with great thankfulness, quoted: 'Thou shalt not be burned; neither shall the flame kindle upon thee' (Isaiah 43: 2).

*　　*　　*

Hugh retired in 1953. He was ready for a rest, for he was then seventy years of age and had been in the demanding business of journalism for fifty-five years, nearly fifty of them in Fleet Street. There is no doubt that the most satisfying were those from 1934 when he served as religious editor of the *News Chronicle*, a post he filled with outstanding success. As a one-time colleague on the paper was to say of Hugh's work as a journalist: 'He worked in Fleet Street and used that worldly thoroughfare with its thundering machines, speeding vans, typewriters and telephones as a loud-speaker to proclaim the good news of the gospel. He was loved, because he was the voice of an authentic prophet of the twentieth century.' (*Stop Press!* by Alfred Angel [Arthur James, Evesham]).

He lived for a further ten years following his retirement and all that time, until weakness just before the end prevented him, he continued to be the tireless traveller, speaker, writer — all his efforts being directed to the promotion of the cause of Christ's Kingdom.

He took a close interest in the little Salvation Army corps at St. Mary Cray, near to where he lived. Often he would attend the Sunday morning holiness meeting there and join in worship with the Salvationists. To Hugh there was something quite special about a Salvation Army holiness meeting and he was always delighted to have the opportunity, which was sometimes afforded him, of conducting one himself.

Brigadier Mrs. Margaret Warner, who was then in charge of the corps, used to visit Hugh's home in the course of her pastoral duties, and she recalls his great courtesy and goodness, and remembers with gratitude his concern for her personally. She was a widow with a young daughter, and had to carry the burden of running the corps alone. He wrote to her just before Christmas 1955:

> The enclosed comes with all good wishes for Christmas to you and your daughter from my wife and myself. While you may have a needy case or two that you would like to help, I would prefer to think that it provided some additional good cheer for you. If I'm not too late with it, how about a chicken?

And that, says Mrs. Warner, was typical of the good, kindly caring man he was.

*　　　*　　　*

There came, however, a serious interruption to all this activity in retirement, an interruption which seemed likely to be permanent. All the signs were that Hugh had reached the end of the road. He gave a full account of those difficult days in his last book, written two years after the event he described, and the account of it is told here, for the most part, in his own words.

In June 1956 he paid a short visit to the West Country, fulfilling a couple of speaking engagements and visiting friends old and new. At the end of the month he returned home to Orpington a little tired but otherwise feeling quite fit. That being 'a little tired' was to become more frequent. Though for some time he kept up his heavy programme of public engagements and coped magnificently with the mass of correspondence which showed no signs of diminishing, the tiredness increased. Soon he began to feel 'not well' and later 'quite ill'. He said nothing to his wife for some time, for he did not want to worry her, and she was far from fit herself. But his condition could not be kept from her indefinitely and when at last she suspected something was quite seriously wrong, and Hugh had to admit there was, she called the doctor. After a thorough check he advised an X-ray examination, and it was clear that he was already convinced that hospital and an operation would have to follow. Hugh was naturally concerned, and about his reaction to the news he later wrote:

In my quiet hour, the following morning, I made an unreserved recommital of myself to Christ,

'The Great Physician now is near,
The sympathising Jesus . . .'

I felt it was true, and I put myself, *for life or death*, entirely in His hands. We did not then know the full seriousness of affairs, but He gave me deliverance from fear that moment. It is not a boast, but a deeply humble and grateful testimony.

Then he put a question: Can we talk of the Lord confirming an agreement in writing? And he asked his readers to consider something which to him was plainly of the greatest significance. Within an hour or two of his recommital a friend was writing a letter to him, It began:

Good morning, dear brother.

You are able to greet this day with joy, I feel sure, knowing the Hand of God is upon you. You have today, 6.55 a.m., gripped afresh the nail-pierced Hand and received new strength and vigour.

Making his record of this Hugh went on:

Don't ask me how she knew, even to the actual time. I cannot explain; I can only record and wonder. I learned to value her prayers when she was a Slum Officer in The Salvation Army and there were times even then when she seemed to have channels of knowledge which passed my comprehension. I had mentioned in a letter to her that I had not been feeling well, and I had also asked for her remembrance in prayer; but here she was abreast of a transaction of which I was thinking as a secret shared only by Him with whom it was completed; and reading her words I knew the peace which is greater than man's understanding.

The X-ray examination revealed a cancer of the pelvirectal junction, about the size of small hen's eggs, pressing on the bowel. Fuller examination and treatment were necessary and Hugh agreed to have them. But the verdict following was so much grimmer. A second, major, operation was urgently necessary. Without it there was little hope. Hugh deferred giving consent for this. He wanted time to pray. Then he would give his decision.

It was made, in fact, next morning (he wrote) in a quiet corner of the hospital grounds. This was a matter of life and death; by God's help I must make no mistake. I was committed to Him, and the feeling was strong within me that I should not have the operation; but I wanted to be sure that the feeling was genuine conviction and not just funk masquerading as faith. So acting on the advice of the hymn, I 'took it to the Lord in prayer', and the help I asked for came flooding in. I was in the Valley, but my Shepherd was with me . . . I could give my decision and fear no evil.

When Hugh communicated his decision not to have the oper-ation the doctor, himself a Christian man and firm believer in the power of prayer, spoke plainly: 'It is my duty to tell you that, if you do not have this operation, I shall not expect to find you alive at Christmas.' But Hugh was sure that Christ could heal him. He was also convinced that his work on earth was not yet finished. His moment of quiet communion with God, as he pondered the grave issue in the secluded corner of the hospital garden, had brought him the assurance that he would not die.

He went home and made steady progress towards the recov-ering of his health. Amazingly, before long he was speaking again in public, and he went on working for Christ for a further seven years, travelling hundreds of miles, addressing meetings here, there and everywhere, and bringing the healing of the gospel to many people. He had been right: in 1956 his work had not been complete, so much more remained to be done, and by God's great grace Hugh was able to do it.

In the book which he wrote to tell the story of his meeting with death, and of his recovery, he gave God the glory as he reaffirmed in print once more his faith in His love and power. He emphasised that he saw his deliverance as the Lord's loving response to the renewal of his own full surrender to the divine purpose. He had thrown open 'his every channel, spiritual, mental and physical, to the full flow of His grace', he said, and the miracle came. For Hugh it was as simple and as profound as that.

But of course, while rejoicing in, and using to the full, the extra time permitted to him to pursue the work he loved, Hugh knew that the end of his life on earth could not be many years delayed, for he had passed his three score years and ten. Six months before his death he had a premonition, which he communicated to his daughter, that his time was near, though he was then as physically fit as any man could expect to be at his age. 'I am not going to be around much longer to trouble you,' he said with that quiet, restrained humour he often displayed, and there was no fear. That would have been impossible in a man who believed so deeply that he was fully possessed by God and that there was a place in heaven prepared for him. He was looking forward to all that was to come.

After a brief illness, during which the doctor had him removed to hospital since, with a sick wife and an invalid daughter, he could not be properly looked after at home, Hugh passed quietly away on Boxing Day 1963. He was in his eighty-first year.

Because of what had been firmly given as the diagnosis of his condition seven years earlier, Elsie requested a post-mortem examination, and the result showed that *there was no trace whatsoever of cancer in any organ of the body.* Had the surgeons of 1956 been mistaken? Had the X-ray plates given a wrong picture? Hugh's wife and friends had no doubts about the matter, nor would Hugh himself have hesitated to state his conviction of it. He had had cancer, but a miracle had been granted him. His complete cure was the work of the Lord.

*　　　*　　　*

Tributes to Hugh's life and work poured into the house at Orpington from many parts of the world, for Hugh and his books were known and appreciated far and wide. *The Times* carried a long obituary which spoke of Hugh's tireless energy in the cause of evangelism, and said that 'he maintained throughout his life a serenity and sense of gentle, kindly humour which helped to make him a much loved man'.

Many Salvationists were present at the funeral service held at All Saints' Church, Orpington. General Wilfred Kitching (R.) paid tribute to 'Big Brother' Hugh, referring to his great interest in the Army's Goodwill work and his value to the Christian cause at large. Officers of the Goodwill Department occupied the choir stalls: Hugh would have liked that.

Later the Army held its own service of 'remembrance and thanksgiving' at the Regent Hall, West End venue for many important Salvationist gatherings. Eloquent appreciation was expressed for the splendid work Hugh had done. General Frederick Coutts sent a message, and Alfred Angel, one of the newspaper reporters on the job at Westminster at the 1928 floods, and Hugh's colleague for many years, paid his own tribute. What would have pleased Hugh particularly was the use in that gathering of the simple chorus he himself had dubbed the 'hop-fields anthem' — 'God is with us all the time . . .'

A memorial service held in London in February was attended by people from the worlds of journalism, broadcasting and religion, and the Lord Bishop of Tonbridge spoke for many when, in the words the Shunammite woman used of the prophet Elisha, according to 2 Kings 4: 9, he said: 'I perceive that this is an holy man of God, which passeth by us continually.'

Hugh would have protested at the application to him of such

a phrase as that. But he would have been quite wrong to do so. The words provide a fitting epitaph. A 'holy man of God' he undoubtedly was.